Food and Beverage Management in the Luxury Hotel Industry

Food and Beverage Management in the Luxury Hotel Industry

Sylvain Boussard

BEP

BUSINESS EXPERT PRESS

Leader in applied, concise business books

Food and Beverage Management in the Luxury Hotel Industry

Cover design by Charlene Kronstedt

Interior design by Exeter Premedia Services Private Ltd., Chennai, India

First published in 2021 by
Business Expert Press, LLC
222 East 46th Street, New York, NY 10017
www.businessexpertpress.com

ISBN-13: 978-1-63742-010-2 (paperback)
ISBN-13: 978-1-63742-011-9 (e-book)

Business Expert Press Tourism and Hospitality Management Collection

Collection ISSN: 2375-9623 (print)
Collection ISSN: 2375-9631 (electronic)

First edition: 2021

10 9 8 7 6 5 4 3 2 1

Description

This book is an introduction to the management of food and beverage operations within a luxury hotel environment. It provides detailed coverage of operational areas within the food and beverage department, based on multiple real industry examples, allowing the reader to grasp the intricacies of the day-to-day running of outlets.

Food and Beverage Management in the Luxury Hotel Industry is a reference for any hospitality management student wishing to gain sufficient knowledge in the subject, to conduct a quantitative and qualitative analysis of the department, through revenue and cost management, and quality audits. It also looks at the various trends shaping the industry today, particularly focusing on sustainability issues and ethical concerns.

Keywords

luxury hotel; management; food and beverage; revenue; hygiene; staff; service; expenses; guest; standards; prime cost; menu; chef; kitchen

Dedication

This book is dedicated to all the amazing persons, fellow hoteliers, chefs, food and beverage directors, general managers, whom I had the opportunity to meet during numerous experiences in the luxury hotel industry, on the four corners of the planet! Thank you for your constant friendship, support, and words of advice.

None of the facets of such a lifetime adventure could have taken place without my parents, for giving me life, education, and openness of mind to undertake this path, and also to Mr. Pacaud, my first English teacher! As I am writing this, I also have a kind thought for my dear school friends Jean-Michel, George, Rolando, and Alexis, who helped me get my early career on the road in Cape Town and Cancun.

To all my readers, present and future, students, professors, food and beverage professionals, business owners, and anyone having an interest in the industry: I wish you pleasure in reading this book, and I hope it will contribute to success and happiness in your current and future ventures in the exciting world of luxury hotel management.

Contents

Introduction

This book blends management techniques with *on-the-field* experiences, in the realm of the luxury hotel industry, particularly focusing on food and beverage operations, seen through the eyes of a hotelier.

Further than the technical aspects, it is also about sharing a passion for the luxury hotel industry at an international level, which began at a rather young age in my case. In my view, being a hotelier is about adopting a lifestyle that offers much more than professional rewards, it is more like an ongoing journey filled with human, cultural, and professional discoveries of all sorts. The main objective of this book is to invite the reader to jump into the reality of managing a day-to-day operation in a luxury resort or hotel.

After more than 20 years of an international career in luxury hospitality, I thought it was time to share some insights and knowledge with the future generations of hoteliers, convey that passion for the hospitality industry, and hopefully open a window into this unique world.

Many details of operational areas within the food and beverage department of a luxury hotel are covered, mostly based on real industry examples and case studies, allowing the reader to grasp the intricacies of the day-to-day running of outlets in a luxury environment.

The main technical aspects of the operation of a food and beverage department are covered in the book, making it a useful reference for any hospitality management student wishing to gain sufficient knowledge in the subject. It enables quantitative and qualitative analysis of the department, through quality audits, and revenue and cost management.

The latest food and beverage trends are presented, particularly focusing on sustainability issues and ethical concerns.

This textbook is aimed at hospitality management students, restaurant managers, and basically anyone who is already working in the luxury hotel industry, at a supervisory level.

It is divided in easy-to-follow sections and acts as a comprehensive guide to all facets of food and beverage activities.

Main topics

Food and beverage management

Luxury hospitality industry

Food and beverage service

Kitchen and stewarding departments

Customer service

Food and beverage cost control

Profit and loss analysis

Key performance indicators

Industry ratios

Keywords

Audit	Efficient	Management	Purchasing
Average check	Executive committee	Margin	Quality
Back of the house	Expenses	Marketing	Ratio
Banqueting	Fast food	Menu analysis	Recipe
Bars	Financial period	Michelin guide	Recipe costing sheet
Beverage	Fixed costs	Mise en place	Recruitment
Brigade	Food and beverage cost control	Net profit	Restaurant
Budget		Payroll	Revenue
Buffet		Non-controllable expenses	Roster
CapEx	Food and beverage director	Operating costs	Salaries
Casual	Forecast	Operations	Sales
Catering	Franchise	Organization	Satisfaction
Chef de partie	Front of the house	Organizational charts	Service
Chef de rang			Set menu
Chef			Silverware

Chafing dish	Gastronomy	Other expenses	Sommelier
Chief steward	Glassware	Outlet	Spoilage
Chinaware	Grooming	Overheads	Staff
Conference	Gross profit	Par stock	Standards
Controllable expenses	Percentage	Pastry	Stars
Controller	Head of department	Percentages	Stock
Cost	Hospitality	Point of sales	Storage
Cost of goods sold – COGS	Hotelier	(POS)	Suppliers
Cost provision	Kitchen	Prime cost	System
Covers	Hygiene	Procedures	Tableware
Critical item	Income	Producer	Teamwork
Customer	Inventory	Production	Training
Cutlery	Job description	Profit and loss	Trend
Department	Key positions	Profitability	Wages
Dishwashing	Kitchen		Waste
Dispense bar	Labor cost		
Distributor	Luxury		
	Maintenance		
	Maître d'hôtel		

Methodology

The textbook is divided in several main sections, gradually familiarizing the reader with the complexity of management activities within the food and beverage department. The main departments involved within food and beverage are presented, and their respective functions are outlined in detail.

Realistic industry case studies and exercises invite the reader(s) to test their own skills and knowledge, and will provide the ability to perform an operational analysis and a *business health check* to any given food and beverage organization.

Each new set of industry terms is introduced in the *Keywords* section at the beginning of each chapter. Furthermore, an industry *Glossary* section is located at the end of the book.

Throughout the book, luxury hospitality stories illustrate the various topics, which range from setting up a catering operation on a luxury train in the Peruvian Andes, to managing a crisis within food and beverage staff on French Polynesia's Bora Bora Island.

Learning Outcomes

- Acquire an understanding of the components of food and beverage in luxury hospitality
- Demonstrate analytical skills on the key functional areas of the food and beverage department
- Understand the structure and organization of any food and beverage operation
- Interpret the main ratios used in the industry and evaluate the impact of management decisions on profitability and efficiency

Prelude

Keywords	
Beverage	Kitchen
Cost	Luxury
Customer	Management
Department	Operation
Dining	Outlet
Director	Professional
Experience	Restaurant
Grooming	Service
Guests	Skills
Hospitality	Staff
Hotelier	

The roots of our passions and what we love today are forged by our childhood experiences and memories; to illustrate this further, I will start by mentioning a few personal facts that ignited my early passion for the luxury hospitality industry.

Strangely enough, my upbringing had no connection whatsoever with the hotel business: my father was a physicist, doing research work at the CERN, the European Center for Nuclear Research on the French-Switzerland border near Geneva. Although very different industries, there was a link between science and the hotel business: multicultural interactions, which is after all the basis of any hotel, even more so in the luxury segment. This is something that we take now for granted, but when I grew up in the 1970s and 1980s, having Chinese or Russian guests at your home was not that common.

My parents often welcomed fellow scientists at our home in the mountains for semi-friendship, semi-professional dinners. My mother, who was and still is an excellent cook, delighted us and my father's colleagues with delicacies such as *gratin dauphinois*, a local potato gratinated with Gruyère or Comté cheese, and many other fantastic dishes: coquilles Saint-Jacques au gratin,[1] coq au vin,[2] far breton,[3] to name a few. In pure French tradition, food and wines would be enjoyed, described, and commented on at great length as they would make it to the table.

My family lived in a wooden chalet, above the city of Gex, in the East of France, and very close to the Swiss border. From a very young age, I was bathed in a mixture of foreign languages, conversations ranging from the new plans for the LEP accelerator[4] to the amount of snow that was falling, and how our guests would make it back home without snow tires!

Perhaps, as a result, my main interest in school was in foreign languages: I strongly believed they would be useful in everyday life, and the future proved me right. I take this opportunity to thank Monsieur Pacaud, my first English teacher, for unknowingly starting me up on a globetrotting path, through the lyrics of *The Beatles*, which we studied in his class.

At age seven, I kept saying I wanted to be a chef; at 14, I was registered on the seven-year waiting list of the prestigious Ecole Hôtelière de Lausanne,[5] with one idea in mind: travel the world.

The *Ecole Hôtelière de Lausanne* Chapter: Perfect Blend of Theory and Practice

Theory or practice? The right blend of the two is very much needed in the luxury hospitality industry, whose success relies heavily on a very specific set of skills.

Aged 17, a few years before joining the school, I remember telling my parents that I just wanted to complete semester one, which focused on kitchen operations, at the Ecole Hôtelière de Lausanne, and then head

---

[1] Oven gratinated scallops in their own shell.

[2] French traditional recipe of chicken braised in Burgundy red wine.

[3] Also named Farz forn, a traditional cake from Brittany, France.

[4] The large electron–positron collider (LEP) was one of the largest particle accelerators ever constructed. It was built at CERN, a multi-national center for research in nuclear and particle physics near Geneva, Switzerland (Wikipedia).

[5] Hospitality management school in Switzerland. It was founded in 1893 and is the oldest hospitality school in the world.

out to discover the world, without finishing my studies. Understandably, they were not that impressed with the idea, but fortunately, I quickly changed my mind a few years later, when I discovered what it meant to be a student there. My first impression as I walked in the school's vast lobby area: extremely serious and focused-looking students, all dressed up in suit and ties, which made me somewhat intimidated, having barely managed to execute my first half Windsor knot[6] a few hours before! Soon enough, I started to realize that appearances are what they are: external signs, which enable one to be as neutral as possible, respecting others and avoiding the risk of offending anyone. This is the reason why, in luxury hospitality, personal presentation, grooming, and uniforms are so important.

During a career in the luxury hotel industry, one will be interacting with guests from all walks of life, from many different cultures, hence the necessity to be as presentable as possible, but without going overboard with the latest fashion statement. This is the most basic but also the most useful thing I have learned at the hotel school, and I have verified its importance time and time over during my professional tenures. Does it mean we should not focus on finance, food and beverage, marketing, communication, front office, and everything else? Well, not quite, but presentation and professional attitude are fundamental ingredients of success in the luxury hospitality industry.

Ecole Hôtelière de Lausanne was for me a real eye opener, a cultural blast, which hit the right buttons in me, I understood and adopted its philosophy straight away. I knew I was about to be a part of a large family and professional network. A member of the *dots on the wall* as I called them: the first thing you could see when entering the school's reception area, was a huge Plexiglas-made world map, literally covered in red and green dots: each one represented an *Ancien*, as the alumni of Ecole Hôtelière de Lausanne are called. The first time I laid my eyes on it I stood there for some time and started daydreaming about all these far away and remote places … I instinctively knew I was in the right place, and I wanted to live my life being a dot on the map.

---

[6] The half-Windsor knot, also known as the single Windsor knot, is a way of tying a necktie, which produces a neat, triangular knot. It is larger than the four-in-hand knot and Pratt knot, but smaller than the Windsor knot (Wikipedia).

A few months later, I was back at school, aged, 14 or 15, for my first interview with the admissions director at the Ecole Hôtelière de Lausanne. A week or two prior to this, I had been asked to send the school a tape, as mp3 or audio files had not yet been invented, to prove that I could speak a reasonable amount of English.

The most intimidating bit for me was that I had to put on a tie for the very first time in my life. Luckily, my father helped me out on that one, and that is when I learned the famous *half-Windsor* technique. Years later, I found out that there existed about a dozen other techniques. Of course, spending those years at Lausanne Hotel School brought much more than grooming standards: self discipline, courtesy and respect of others, attention to details, and over anything else, a constant strive to excellence. The school is based on many hours of practice in all the departments of a hotel; it is a little bit like being in a laboratory; each task can be rehearsed, mistakes are made, and instant feedback obtained from the instructors. I found this method to be the best to prepare oneself for the realities of hotel operations.

Hotelier, a Lifestyle

Although luxury hospitality management relies on many technical skills, from managing inventories to calculating cost of sales ratios, or training staff on wine opening, the most important and relevant skills are the ones developed every day on the field. Interpersonal skills such as care spirit and empathy, but also a good dose of resilience and other personal attitude traits that cannot be taught in a book, but rather acquired by situational experiences. Let us have a look further at what is required to become a successful hotelier in a luxury environment.

Strictly speaking, most of the basic skills are not extremely complex ones, even a chef in a fine dining-restaurant, or a pastry chef, will acquire most of their knowledge through experience, training, and dedication. Of course, it may take years to become an experienced sommelier, through layers of wine knowledge acquired day after day, service after service. It also requires passion, patience, resilience, and a will to wander into the unknown, out of one's comfort zone. Traveling and working in many different cultures can greatly help to achieve this, and the luxury hotel job market usually values candidates with international experience.

If you are seeking a calibrated life, without too many surprises and discoveries, then perhaps, the hotel industry is not the greatest choice, but on the other hand, if you are interested in people and providing them with well-being, if you are adventurous and looking for experiences in very diverse cultures, then this could be the right kind of occupation for you.

Traveling as a visitor is one thing, but getting to stay in very different countries and experience numerous cultures, can be seen as a great advantage for certain professionals, although it is not always the easiest lifestyle to adopt, especially for professionals traveling with families.

For certain hoteliers, and this is my case, it feels as a privilege to live a unique life and to be able to start all over again in a new country. Based on my own observations, in luxury hotel chains, most management positions will remain in one post between two and three years, before being offered a transfer to another business outlet, sometimes on the other side of the planet. I have witnessed many colleagues traveling in such a way from Europe to America, then onto Asia, and later to the Middle East, in the span of a decade or less.

Another particularity of the luxury hospitality industry is its strong, supportive, and reliable professional network; it is almost like a brotherhood around the world. Perhaps, it has to do with the passion most hoteliers put into their daily tasks, most work colleagues will help each other throughout their careers. After all, this is one of the few industries in which you work 12 hours a day on average, weekends, and public holidays, and it does not feel so much as a job, as you experience exciting situations, get involved in many great projects, meet interesting people all over the world, get to live in beautiful surroundings, and get paid for it all. In the last 22 years, I lived in 12 countries, giving me the feeling of living many different lives.

Human interaction, in our times of artificial intelligence and robots, is also what makes working in the luxury hotel industry attractive and challenging. There are nowadays not so many industries left where you can still meet and interact with human beings from all walks of life and social conditions. The food and beverage teams I was responsible for during my career ranged between 100 or 200 members of staff, and it would be almost impossible to calculate the number of guests I have met on any day, from so many nationalities, with so many different needs and expectations. Needless to say, machines are not yet to replace humans, at least in luxury hotels.

Coming back to the network aspect in the hotel industry, here is an example of how it can help in a job search, with a bit of luck too: freshly graduated from hotel school, I was called for military duties in France, for a year, during which my schoolmates were starting their respective careers in different corners of the world.

After having completed my military service, I contacted a hotel near Geneva, where I had been training during my school years, and got a six-month contract as a night auditor, in the reception area. This allowed me to have some free time during the day to begin my international job search. Unfortunately, I would get very few replies, and when they came, most of them sounded like this: "Unfortunately you don't have enough experience for the position …," which made me wonder, how can I get experience if I always get this kind of answer?

I decided to call my good-old school friend, George, a Greek student who was in my work group at school: he had started his career in a luxury hotel in South Africa. After our conversation, I thought about going there to take a look for myself, instead of sending more application letters. On January 1, 1992, my two suitcases were ready for the flight to Cape Town, and George kindly let me stay in his flat for a few days until I got settled.

As soon as I arrived, he also connected me with a few key people in restaurants and hotels in the area, and as a result, two weeks later I had my first job as a restaurant manager at *Signatures*, a California-inspired fine-dining restaurant, with a Swiss Ecole Hôtelière de Lausanne alumnus behind the stoves.

And, that is how the whole travel bug really got me, and never really left since then.

Small World

As mentioned earlier, traveling builds international experience, which is highly valued in the luxury hospitality industry: the more cultures you know, the more languages you speak, and the better equipped you are for a successful career in the industry, interacting with guests and staff from very distinct cultures.

For anyone interested in becoming a *citizen of the world*, being an international hotelier in luxury hospitality is a real gift: you get to meet all kinds of people, from kings to rock stars, provide them with enjoyable experiences, and hopefully exceed their expectations (which is the basic goal of any luxury hospitality organization). Some of the most challenging, but also highly rewarding service experiences, include catering for world-class famous events, such as the Cumbre de Rio in Peru. This particular event took place in 2003 and brought together 19 Latin American presidents in Cusco and Lima (see Chapter 3, customer service and crisis management, *Avoid a diplomatic incident, know your menu*). The hotelier has to combine various skills very similar to scenario writing, stage planning, and producing, all this in very diverse settings, often in dream locations. It can definitely be an adventurous enterprise, without a day similar to the other!

Having said that, it is not comfortable and fun every day, and like in any human enterprise, conflicts often arise. In my experience, around 50 percent of my time was dedicated to managing those and finding solutions. It could be an internal conflict with staff, or with guests, or a combination of both at the same time. For example, many members of staff would like to have weekends off, but it is not always possible, and this can lead to disagreements. There are also guest complaints arising from staff attitude, which could be inappropriate in their eyes, or conflicts caused by language barriers or communication issues. Whatever the cause, it is management's duty to ensure a swift and efficient resolution of complaints, which involves dealing with the guests while they are staying at the hotel. On the positive side, that is one of the best aspects of working in the luxury hospitality industry: find solutions to exceed guest's expectations and be rewarded by a smile on someone's face!

One of the greatest aspects of having management experience in luxury hotel operations is that it is transposable to any other hotel operation, regardless of its location. It is a great advantage for managers who want to move around the planet: the world becomes smaller each day, and it is quite common to cross paths with former colleagues within the industry.

Dreams, Intuitions, Foreign Languages

After having enjoyed a few years in Cape Town, I trusted my intuition and flew to Mexico, another member of my Ecole Hôtelière de Lausanne workgroup was working for a large international hotel chain there, so I thought I could repeat South Africa's success story and get a work contract within a few weeks' time. I once again packed a few suitcases, and I was on my way, impatient to start a new life learning Spanish while honing my management skills. As my dream was to be an international hotelier, I undoubtedly needed to speak a second foreign language, and the best way to learn it, as I was about to find out, was the hard way.

As in my previous job-seeking experience, I experienced a low answer rate to job applications, and still the mention of not having enough experience. Since then, and all throughout my professional activities, I have made a point of consistently answering prospective candidates, at least to thank them for taking the time to write. After all, with the modern communication tools at our disposal, answering an e-mail takes about five seconds, which surely can fit in any schedule, no matter how busy it is. Also, you may cross paths with an applicant sooner than you think, the hotel world being so small, so "treat others as you'd like to be treated" works well!

Moving to Mexico gave me the opportunity to learn something very useful: that it usually pays to be bold, perseverant, and to take measured risks. I did not speak more than a few words of Spanish and was without the shadow of a job lead when I embarked on the bus to Cancun, in the southern part of the country, from Cuernavaca, one of Mexico City's most pleasant suburbs. There, I had been hosted by Rolando, my schoolmate from the Ecole Hôtelière de Lausanne. I was determined to get a job in one of the many luxury hotels of this American-inspired Mexican tourism hub. Virtually, all the luxury chains are represented in Cancun, from the Ritz Carlton to Mandarin Oriental and Hyatt International hotels. For the next two months, I would roam up and down the *Zona hotelera*,[7] knocking on many doors, and as a result, I succeeded in getting a few recruitment interviews, learning Spanish on-the-go.

Despite my efforts, there was no job in sight. As my financial situation starting to decline, and my tourist visa was coming to an end, I decided to try my luck in Merida, capital of Yucatan State, a three-hour bus ride from Cancun. Merida's luxury hotels' offer was quite simple: the newly built Hyatt Regency, Fiesta Americana hotel, and a somewhat rundown Holiday Inn, all facing each other on Avenida Colon.[8]

Figure P.1 Quiet provincial capital of Yucatan State, Merida, Mexico

Fiesta Americana's food and beverage manager advised me to come back in a couple of months, as they had nothing available for the time being. The Hyatt Regency's food and beverage manager was in a meeting, so I left him a message, without expecting too much as my return bus ride was scheduled the same evening that day. Back in my hotel, and ready to check out, I was beginning to wonder if my plan to just show up in Mexico, get a job, and learn Spanish had perhaps been too ambitious. At that very moment, the phone rang at the reception, and I saw the receptionist looking at me while answering, "Yes, he is here, hold

---

[7] Hotel zone of Cancun.
[8] Merida's central avenue.

on please, I will put you through." It was the Hyatt's food and beverage manager, and a few minutes later, I was on my way back to the hotel for a job interview, literally minutes before I was to catch my six o'clock bus back to Cancun, which would have brought an end to the *Mexico Project*.

By mere coincidence, the Swiss food and beverage manager at the Hyatt was part of my professional network, another Ecole Hôtelière de Lausanne alumnus, another *dot* on the wall! The interview ended up successfully, as I got offered a job as assistant banqueting manager; I was thrilled, as this meant I could carry on with an international career in food and beverage management, in the luxury hotel industry.

Before embarking on this journey through the book, it is necessary to describe the many facets of the luxury hospitality industry, in order to define it precisely. This will be the object of the next chapter, *Luxury Hospitality*.

CHAPTER 1

Luxury Hospitality

Keywords	
Career	Management
Customer	Resort
Dining	Service
Grooming	Standards
Hotelier	Stars
Location	

As this book highlights food and beverage management in luxury establishments, the first question to be addressed is: what is a luxury hotel made of?

Today, the word luxury has been so overused that it is sometimes quite complicated for the customer to understand what to expect in terms of service and facilities: for example, a five-star hotel in Panama or Hong Kong may differ from one another completely, in terms of quality of service, facilities, pricing, and many other aspects.

And, what to say of countries such as France that have altogether different classification systems such as palaces? To make things even more complicated, some countries mostly rely on guest comments, while again, in France's example, strict regulations must be followed in order to access a certain level of stars; those are determined by the Minister of Tourism through *Atout France*.[1]

---

[1] France Tourism Development Agency, which promotes the country as a tourist destination. It also oversees the attribution of stars to hotels, following strict regulations.

Based on years of observations and numerous interactions with luxury hotel guests, I can safely say that luxury is made of three main components:

- The *staff*. Without their efforts and willingness to please others, there simply cannot be any positive guest experience.
- The *hotel's facilities*: Just like a luxury car is expected to have leather seats and many other quality features, a luxury hotel definitely needs to have certain physical assets that differentiates it from a budget or three-star hotel.
- Clearly defined *processes* that constantly and consistently exceed customers' expectations, they are referred to as *standards* in the hospitality industry.

Just as in a kitchen recipe, high-quality ingredients are necessary to obtain a great result, but the right mix and perfect execution of the recipe are also key factors for success.

Once the three ingredients are all in place, staff, facilities and processes, the ability to transform these into luxury will greatly depend on the management team in place. Following are the detailed descriptions and examples of the three ingredients for success.

Staff

A beautifully equipped hotel with a spa, latest in-room technology, fine-dining restaurant, 24-hour room service, which has poorly or no trained personnel, or even worse, unwelcoming and demotivated staff, may be presented in its brochure or website as a luxury establishment, but will not result in a luxury guest experience.

Staffing is the most important attribute of any luxury hotel or restaurant operation; it is also the most complex *mix* to achieve. Training and experience are only part of the equation. As written earlier, and I know most of my colleagues in the luxury hotel business agree with me: attitude prevails over skills.

A career in the luxury hotel business, which is highly demanding, is simply not suited for everyone. Let us face it, to accomplish a luxury service and exceed guests' expectations is not an easy thing to achieve: it requires repetition, patience, learning through failure, and a great amount of resilience. One thing a hotelier must always keep in mind is that luxury hospitality is essentially a people-to-people business, and hotel guests pay a premium price to receive a consistent high-quality service. Every one of us may have good days and not so good days, but our main duty as hoteliers is to ensure our guests receive an excellent service throughout their stay, no matter the situation or the hour of the day. Individual attitude and predisposition, therefore, play an enormous role in achieving guest satisfaction. In order to deliver consistent service quality, the best way is to imagine you are going on stage every time you start a shift: focus, the stage is all yours, perform as best as you can, put on your best smile! Many times, as described in the short stories throughout the book, improvisation will be required, it is part of the game, and this is how experience is gained.

Being open to others and their distinctive cultures, being empathetic, with a built-in desire to please, not afraid to give a smile away even when under enormous pressure: those are the basic attributes required for anyone wishing to succeed in a career in the luxury hotel industry.

These points bring us to the subject of managing interviews of potential candidates: there are certain staff attributes that should be sought after, regardless of the number of years one has worked in five-star hotel or palace, although it does have its importance too. Following is a non-exhaustive list, in order of importance:

- *On stage* attitude.
- Desire to please others.
- Efficiency: Acquire a *Swiss knife* approach to challenges, possess a solution-driven mind is a required quality, when most of the concept of guest service is based on finding ways to resolve issues that inevitably arise during hotel stays.
- Impeccable grooming and personal presentation.
- Well-developed communication skills.
- Honesty, integrity.
- Ability to work in multicultural teams.
- Knowledge of different languages.

- Highly developed memory skills, useful to remember repeat guests and greet them by their name.
- Discretion, as guest contacts are numerous. Housekeeping staff, for example, should take great care when handling personal belongings in the guest's room. The same could be said about restaurant waiters who should keep a neutral distance when overhearing personal conversations.

Figure 1.1 Grooming and personnel presentation, one of luxury hospitality's basics

Facilities

Facilities include many important features of any luxury hotel, starting with a prime location. As Ellsworth Statler, father of the modern hotel industry, said, there are three important factors in the hotel business: location, location, and … location.[2] The building quality, as well as the upkeeping of its public areas, will also be determinant. Here are some international standards of facilities expected in a luxury hospitality establishment:

---

[2] https://rockcheetah.com/blog/hotel/a-new-location-location-location-for-the-hotel-industry/

Enhanced Room Features

- King-sized bed is the norm, with a firm mattress and natural fiber sheets.
- At least two generous and fluffy pillows, made of natural fibers. Many luxury hotels offer pillow menus, enabling the guest to choose from different grades of firmness and sizes.
- Large windows, featuring natural lighting, high-quality curtains blocking out the light for a peaceful sleep.
- The room should be spacious enough, for instance, a room at the Plaza Athénée in Paris is 270 square feet.[3]
- Design and furnishings should be of high quality and well maintained.
- Air control should be silent and efficient. In some high-altitude hotels, oxygen is even piped into the rooms at guest's request, for an additional fee. This is the case at the Hotel Monasterio in Cusco, Peru, located in the Andes, at 11,000 feet altitude.

Figure 1.2 Standard room at Belmond Hotel Monasterio, Cusco, Peru

---

[3] https://dorchestercollection.com/en/paris/hotel-plaza-athenee/rooms-suites/classic-guestroom/

- Overall, there should not be any cheap touches, and original art should be displayed on the walls.
- Special attention to small aesthetics details is key too, for example, no electric cables should be visible.
- Technology: Use of technology is a must have for any modern luxury hotel, with one main goal in mind: increasing the guest's comfort and security. There are numerous examples of technology use in the luxury industry: radio frequency identification (RFID) room keys, central control of air conditioning, heating units and lighting, vocal assistants, and many others.
- Storage space: There should be a dedicated space for storage of the guest's personal belongings, including an electronic personal safe, and quality hangers, not the anti-theft ones, or made of thin plastic.
- A comfortable reading chair should be available, as well as a desk and quality stationary.

Figure 1.3 Suite furniture at the Conrad Maldives Rangali Island

- An expresso coffee maker, with a choice of premium coffee, including decaffeinated, and a selection of whole-leaf premium teas.
- A full length mirror.
- Quality bathrobes and slippers.

Figure 1.4 A private telescope awaits each suite guest at the Conrad Maldives Rangali Island

Bathroom

- Enough space should be available.
- Marble or tiles without chips and regularly polished.
- A bathtub, which should large enough to comfortably accommodate two guests.
- A high-quality shower, with strong water pressure and easy-to-operate temperature controls.
- Luxury branded amenities, including bar soap.
- An effective ventilation.
- Double sinks.
- High-quality terrycloth, and large towels.
- Bidets for Europe, toto toilet in Asia.

Figure 1.5 Stylish bathroom at Conrad Maldives Rangali Island

Guest Activities

Activities that are proposed in a luxury hotel, with free or paying access, are also a key factor for the guest. Here are the most common ones found in five-star hotels and palaces:

- Access to a fitness center, including a spa, gym, and a heated swimming pool
- A concierge service, a guest relation service department
- A main lobby, with access to free Wi-Fi
- Free and easy to operate Wi-Fi, available throughout the property
- Laundry and dry-cleaning service available 24 hours a day
- Babysitting and pet sitting service available 24 hours a day
- Outstanding dining, featuring modern and updated food and beverage concepts
- A great breakfast, included in the room rate
- A 24-hour room service
- Complimentary touches: Free coffee in lobby, early check in or late check out, use of fitness center, free local phone calls

Figure 1.6 Private swimming pool at the Conrad Maldives Rangali Island

Processes

The hospitality industry, in pursuit of permanent consistency, relies on quality standards that help ensure guest service processes are carried out in a systematic way. The best example in the luxury industry is a worldwide used set of standards called the *Leading Hotels of the World* quality assurance.[4]

Common service standards in luxury hotels

- Luggage delivered in room in less than 10 minutes after the check in
- Express check in and check out available
- Turndown service
- 24-hour efficient room service, with a complete food and beverage offer
- Call guest by their last name
- Answer the phone in less than three rings
- Serve a main dish no more than 15 minutes after it has been ordered

The goal of these standards is to maximize guest satisfaction, through effortless planning: room reservation processes, check in and check out procedures are made the simplest possible for the guest. The ultimate luxury resource nowadays is time, and luxury travelers agree to pay a premium price to avoid waiting in line or filling paperwork.

Renowned luxury hotels around the world

The Americas	Europe
• The Pierre, New York City	• Hotel Peninsula Paris, France
• The Copacabana Palace, Rio de Janeiro, Brazil	• The Dorchester London, United Kingdom
• Hotel Monasterio, Cusco, Peru	• Belmond Cipriani Hotel Venice, Italy
• The Beverly Hills Hotel, Los Angeles	• Beau Rivage Palace, Lausanne, Switzerland
• Palau Duhau, Park Hyatt Buenos Aires, Argentina	• Hotel Adlon Kempinski Berlin, Germany

[4] The Leading Hotels of the World established its product and service standards through Leading QualityAssurance, a company that conducts anonymous property inspections for the world's most prestigious hospitality organizations. The detailed point system is designed to cover all phases of the guest experience, from making a reservation to checking out, including every aspect of the property itself from reception, to the back of the house. https://lhw.com/corporate/standards

Asia Pacific	Africa and Middle East
• Amman Kyoto, Japan	• Burj Al Arab, Dubai
• The Peninsula, Hong Kong	• Six Senses Zighy Bay, Oman
• The Empire Hotel, Brunei	• Belmond Mount Nelson,
• Shangri-La Kuala Lumpur,	Cape Town, South Africa
Malaysia	• Mandarin Oriental
• Bulgari hotel Beijing, China	Marrakech, Morocco
	• Four Seasons Riyadh at
	Kingdom Centre, Saudi Arabia

Figure 1.7 Airport transfers in style, to and from The Peninsula Paris

Luxury hospitality's inside story: the birth of a luxury hotel, making of a Maldivian pearl

Ask any hotelier about opening luxury hotels, the answer will probably be that it is one of the most interesting experiences one can have, but also the most challenging. A million things need to be checked, numerous deadlines have to be respected, in order to be able to offer a finished luxury product, and a corresponding set of services, on the announced opening date, as the first guests check in.

Figure 1.8 First foundations of the future luxury Vilamendhoo Island Resort

That is far from easy to achieve, and even more so in remote locations such as the Maldives,[5] a unique luxury destination in the Indian Ocean, made up of hundreds of islands, which are separated by hours of transportation, either by boat or sea plane. There are many hurdles on the path to the opening of a new hotel. For example, keeping the tight construction deadlines, getting the construction materials to the site, selecting and purchasing the equipment and furniture, recruiting the staff prior to the opening, form the most important ones. In addition to these challenges found in any *conventional* hotel opening, resorts

[5] Maldives, officially the Republic of Maldives, is a small archipelagic island country in South Asia, situated in the Arabian Sea of the Indian Ocean. It lies southwest of Sri Lanka and India, about 700 kilometres (430 miles) from the Asian continent's mainland. The chain of 26 atolls stretches from Ihavandhippolhu Atoll in the north to Addu Atoll in the south to the Equator. Comprising a territory spanning roughly 298 square kilometres (115 square miles), the Maldives is one of the world's most geographically dispersed sovereign states as well as the smallest Asian country by land area and population (Wikipedia).

in the Maldives are built on very small areas of sand, in the middle of the ocean. This explains why Maldivian resorts are mostly made out of wood, a material that is much lighter than cement and bricks. This has an advantage, as wooden structures usually take much less time to build than concrete made structures. For example, The Vilamendhoo Island Resort, located in the South Ari island atoll, was built in just over a year, a record amount of time for building any hotel structure.

In the Maldives, there are no guests walking in the hotel without a reservation, or *walk-ins* as they are called in the industry, so independently owned establishments and chains rely very heavily on travel agencies and tour operators. Their main role is to sell rooms; hence, their concerns are not with the day-to-day construction work. Contracts are signed between hotel chains and tour operators, and the greatest possible number of hotel rooms are booked months ahead of time. Penalties for canceling or changing guest dates of stay are usually very steep, so most hoteliers will have to honor them, even if the hotel is halfway built. That was the case in the example described in this story.

Vilamendhoo Island Resort is set on a 3,000 by 600 feet strip of sand, and offers 220 rooms, spread out on and around the tiny island. On the opening day, only about half the rooms were built, so there was no other choice but to split the island in two: one side for guests and the other side for construction workers.

As you can imagine, the two sides did not blend very well, and understandably, many guests complained of the noise and the lack of access to half of the island, and rightfully rated the hotel below luxury standards!

The main lesson learned out of this experience, which is easy to write but far harder to actually achieve: when planning a hotel opening, always allow for some consequent buffer time, as trying to fill up a hotel or restaurant when it is only partly built is not only an operational nightmare, but can also have a devastating effect on your reputation and image.

It will also bring unnecessary stress on your opening team, having to deal with many—justified—customer complaints.

Figure 1.9 The 220-room luxury resort on Vilamendhoo island

Now that we have defined the main attributes of a luxury hotel, it is time to take a detailed look at the food and beverage industry.

CHAPTER 2

The Food and Beverage Industry

Keywords		
Catering	Health	Suppliers
Chain	Local	Sustainability
Cuisine	Menu	Technological
Environment	Michelin	Trend
Experience	Nutrition	Value
Fine dining	Organic	Vegan
Gastronomy	Producers	

The food and beverage industry is a vast and diversified sector, including private and public-sector establishments, and ranging from small independently owned units to international corporations managing global brands, from oil rig catering to three-starred Michelin restaurants in the world's most luxurious palaces.

Due to the fact that there is no single definition of what should be included in the food and beverage industry, it is rather difficult to obtain consistent statistics. Nevertheless, the National Restaurant Association has developed, over the years, a consistent set of indicators for the United States, which gives an idea of the size of the industry: according to the information shared by their website, for 2019, the economic value of the commercial restaurant industry in the United States was a projected revenue of over 860 billion U.S. dollars, equivalent to about 4 percent of the country's gross domestic product.[1]

---

[1] https://restaurant.org/articles/news/association-report-analyzes-industry-trends

Still according to those 2019 indicators, an estimated one million restaurants operate in the United States, representing in terms of employment, more than 15 million jobs, or one of every 10 Americans.[2] Although, restaurant employment is still perceived as something you would get into for the holidays or while studying as part time job. Six in 10 adults in the United States have worked in the industry at some point, and one out of three Americans got their first employment experience in a restaurant.

As I am writing these lines, the huge impact the Covid-19 is having on the hospitality industry is being evaluated. According to the latest survey conducted by the National Restaurant Association, out of more than 6,500 restaurant operators across the United States:[3]

- More than eight million restaurant employees have already been laid off
- Two out of three restaurant employees have lost their jobs
- The industry's losses are expected to reach 240 billion U.S. dollars by the end of 2020
- Four in 10 restaurants were already closed by April 2020

It remains a very labor-focused industry, as food and beverage service can still not be easily replicated by robots, although there are already many examples of fully automated restaurants in China, Japan, and Europe. The value of the restaurant industry in employment terms is all the more important as it concerns jobs that cannot be relocated and that a great number of people are able to do.

It is also a sector offering many growth opportunities: as many as nine managers out of 10 have started their career in entry-level positions, such as dishwashers or bus persons. Nonetheless, the restaurant industry today is facing a number of challenges that it needs to address, in order to ensure long-term dynamism.

The first challenge lies in the performance of those who work in the industry, especially the smaller businesses, faced with costs, specifically

---

[2] https://restaurant.org/articles/news/association-report-analyzes-industry-trends
[3] https://restaurant.org/manage-my-restaurant/business-operations/covid19/research/industry-research

labor costs, which are constantly increasing. The second challenge revolves around the necessity to understand the evolutions in consumer trends, in order to be able to adapt to them.

Those in the industry, therefore, need to target their customers, in terms of price, type of meal (pleasure or necessity), the kind of experience customers are seeking, levels of quality and so on, and to constantly adapt according to customers' demands. The third challenge is innovation; making the most of current innovations is a significant means of gaining in competitiveness, attractiveness, performance, and ultimately, profitability.

Classification of Food and Beverage Operations
The food service industry—a world of diversity[4,5,6,7]

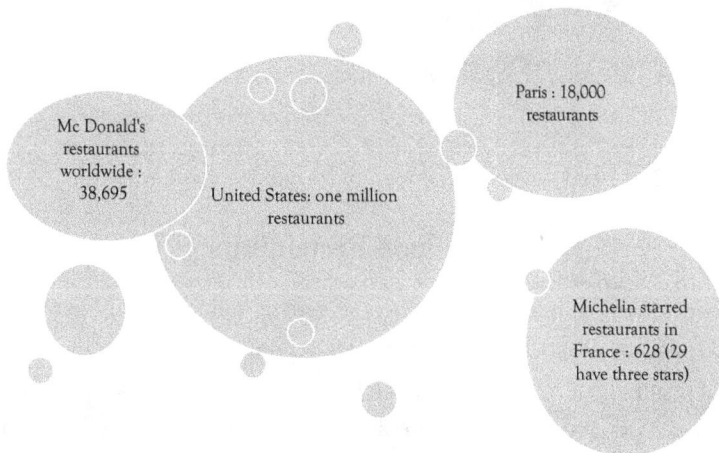

Figure 2.1 Estimation of the number of restaurants (pre-Covid-19)

---

[4] https://statista.com/statistics/219454/mcdonalds-restaurants-worldwide/2019
[5] National Restaurant Association, Industry factbook 2019. https://restaurant.org/downloads/pdfs/research/soi/restaurant_industry_fact_sheet_2019.pdf
[6] Includes Paris and suburbs. https://business.lesechos.fr/entrepreneurs/franchise/efra-00048312-la-restauration-en-france-les-chiffres-du-secteur-203996.php
[7] https://guide.michelin.com/fr/fr/article/dining-out/guide-michelin-france-la-liste-complete-des-etoiles 2020

Management and Ownership Structures

Food and beverage operations are characterized by their diversity, ranging from the café on the corner, independently owned and run, to a trans-continental company such as Sodexo or Compass, operating sites that produce thousands of meals a day.

There are no simple boundaries of the various sectors, and many times, a restaurant or catering operation will fall in more than one classification.

Following is a general classification by type of management or ownership structures.

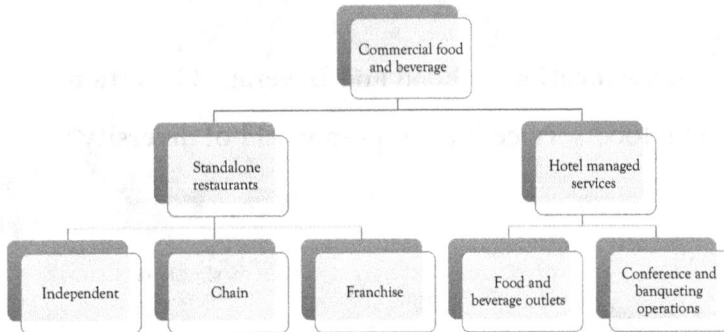

Figure 2.2 Food service classification by management type

Standalone Restaurants

Standalone restaurants, catering to the general public, mostly fit in the independent or chain categories. Franchises are very common in restaurant chain organizations and are ran by independent owners, called franchisees. In this commercial setup, the restaurant chain acts as a franchisor (owner of the brand), delivering franchise rights to the franchisee. In order to use a commercial brand, such as McDonald's, a franchisee will pay a monthly fee, or a percentage of sales to the franchisor. The franchisee then obtains the right to use the brand's logo, benefitiates from marketing strategies deployed by the brand, and has access to the brand's products through a network of approved suppliers.

Hotel Managed Services

Food and beverage hotel-managed services include a vast choice of ventures, which will be developed in great length throughout the next chapters. Two main categories can be identified within hotel managed services:

- Food and beverage outlets: they can be anything from a fine-dining restaurant to a 24-hour room service operation, or a beach bar offering cocktails and snacks (see Section *Food and beverage outlets*).
- Conference and banqueting operations: they differ greatly from the outlets category, in terms of structural organization, staffing, revenue, and cost structure. Each of these points will be treated further in a dedicated section, "Banqueting, meetings and conference department."

Main Categories of Commercial Food and Beverage Establishments

The industry is made of many different types of establishments:

- Standalone restaurants (fine dining, casual, specialty, themed)
- Hotel-managed services (food and beverage outlets, conference, and banqueting)
- Fast-food outlets
- Snack bars, coffee shops
- Pubs, wine bars
- Clubs, service, and sporting
- Retail stores
- Reception centers catering for weddings and conventions
- Events, conferences, exhibitions
- Catering (in-house or off-premises)

This list is by no means exhaustive, as this is a sector constantly evolving and reinventing itself. Furthermore, many establishments often fall in more than one category (e.g., a themed specialty cuisine could also be fast-food outlet).

Family or Casual Style

Also known as casual-style dining, this is a type of restaurant where food is placed in the center of the table so that all guests have access to the dishes. Many Asian concepts, such as Thai, Chinese, and so on, feature this style of service; it is also common with Latin American cuisine, for example, Mexican botanas. In this type of establishment, prices are medium range, portions are usually large, and the settings are comfortable and inviting. Dishes are usually brought to the table by the service staff. Examples in the United States are chain operations such as Chipotle or Applebee's.

Fine Dining

Fine-dining restaurants include a wide range of establishments, such as a theme restaurant within a hotel (food and beverage outlet) or a Michelin-starred independent restaurant. Selling prices are consequently higher than in the other categories: as a rule of thumb, for each Michelin star, the average spent by guest on food alone is around 100 U.S. dollars. Another characteristic of fine-dining restaurants is higher overheads. In this type of establishment, the main focus is on the menu, the service, and the atmosphere. In order to achieve this high quality, operating equipment such as glassware, cutlery, chinaware, or linen is used, and recruitment will target the most skilled staff on the job market. The wine selection is a very important feature of a fine-dining restaurant; it can offer up to thousands of wines, for example, La Tour d'Argent in Paris has 320,000 bottles in its cellar![8] The fine-dining restaurant, most of all, will reflect the chef's personality, with great attention to details, and may feature a very wide variety of cuisines: ethnic, seasonal, organic, or local.

Two main categories of menus are usually offered, à la carte and prix fixe.

À La Carte

Each item is individually priced, and the guest chooses from a list divided into sections (fish, meat, pasta, and so on).

Prix Fixe Menus

Menus are prearranged (starter, main course, dessert, for example), in two, three, or more courses, and the selling prices are set for the different menus.

---

[8] https://tourdargent.com/en/the-wine-cellar/

Figure 2.3 Michelin-starred La Tour d'Argent restaurant in Paris

Café and Bistro

Cafés generally offer table service, although not as sophisticated as in the fine-dining category. Menus are usually centered around coffee, sandwiches, and pastries. Most cafés and bistrots propose *formulas* or set menus at lunchtime. In certain locations, such as in France or Italy, outdoor seating on terraces is another trademark of cafés. Bistros originate from France and are similar to cafés although offering a wider range of dishes. In the past few years, the *bistronomy* trend has emerged, a crossover between bistro and gastronomy.

Figure 2.4 Café in Paris

Buffet Restaurant

The buffet has a French origin, dating back to the 16th century. It features self-service from a wide variety of food offerings. It is often proposed for special occasions, such as weddings or conferences. As a large selection of food is on display, a buffet is not suitable for a small group of guests, as it may be unprofitable. Based on my observations, a buffet will start generating profit for groups of 30 or more. From a service perspective, it is also much more practical and faster than à la carte, as many guests can help themselves simultaneously; it is, therefore, quite common for international medium- to large-sized hotels to offer a breakfast buffet to their guests. Prime cost is also usually lower than in other types of operations. A great variety of styles is found within the buffet category: all you can eat, cafeteria style, catered buffet, breakfast buffets, ethnic, and themed.

Despite its many advantages, the buffet concept will have to reinvent itself in the next years, due to the new social distancing norms brought on by Covid-19. This will, at the very least, imply restrictions in the number of dishes presented, reinforced cleaning protocols, and effective crowd control.

Figure 2.5 Buffet restaurant at the Empire Hotel in Brunei

Food Truck

Food trucks are one of food and beverage's industry latest trends. The past few years have seen an increased development of food trucks all over the world. They feature a wide variety of concepts, from Venezuelan arepas to foie gras, and offer many advantages to the operator or owner:

- Lower investment than in a *classical* brick-and-mortar restaurant: from 50 to 80,000 U.S. dollars on average
- Low-operating costs: rent, staff, utilities
- High visibility on social media
- Greater flexibility

Figure 2.6 Food truck in Saint Petersburg, Russia

Fast-Food Restaurant

This sector is characterized by the presence of many chains, most of them operated through franchises.

The growth of the fast-food restaurant sector has been steady since the 1970s, when global sales was around six billion U.S. dollars. The latest estimates worldwide indicate global sales of 570 billion U.S. dollars, with 200 billion U.S. dollars in the United States alone. The annual business growth is around 2.5 percent, and 50 million fast-food meals are served daily in the United States.[9] Many concepts have been developed within this sector: fast-casual, fast-good, specialty, themed, ethnic, and so on.

---

[9] https://franchisehelp.com/industry-reports/fast-food-industry-analysis-2020-cost-trends/

Fast-Casual Restaurant

Similar to fast-food concepts, the fast-casual restaurant features quick service with quality ingredients and a convenient sit-down atmosphere. A fast-casual restaurant's average check per guest is usually around 30 percent higher than in fast-food operations.

Figure 2.7 Fast-casual restaurant in Paris 10th district

Popup Restaurant

This is a rather recent form of food and beverage operation, very versatile and featuring reduced opening costs. A popup restaurant is by definition not a permanent venture; as such, it can be a solution for renovation or relocation of a main business. Chefs may also use this formula to experiment a new concept, as a *sample restaurant* for a limited time, before actually opening the *real* restaurant. Special events such as *Dinner in the sky*,[10] *Underground dining*,[11] or *Raw almond frozen lake dinner*[12]

---

[10] Dinner in the Sky is a Belgian-based novelty restaurant service, which uses a crane to hoist its diners, table, and waiting staff 150 feet (46 m) into the air. Forbes magazine called it one of the world's 10 most unusual restaurants. Dinner in the Sky has mobile services available in 15 nations and has operations in various cities, including Paris, and Las Vegas. https://dinnerinthesky.com

[11] https://underground-dining.co.uk

[12] http://farandwide.much.com/raw-almond-frozen-lake-dinner/

are a few examples of the infinite possibilities offered by popup restaurants. In fact, just about any location can host a popup restaurant, provided the necessary authorizations are obtained and access to utilities is secured. Operational challenges, such as utilities, staff recruitment, training, and logistics, need to be carefully assessed before undertaking such a project.

Figure 2.8 Popup restaurant, setup and ran by students of culinary school Le Cordon Bleu, Paris

Luxury hospitality's inside story: Andean meals on wheels, setting up Hiram Bingham's luxury catering service

Let us now embark on a gastronomical journey and examine the particularities of a moving restaurant, onboard the Hiram Bingham train,[13] which follows the sacred path of the Incas, from Cusco to the citadel of Machu Picchu in Peru.

---

[13] Luxury train operated by Belmond, operating daily return trips from Cusco to Machu Picchu in Peru.

Another great adventure, and challenge while working with Belmond hotels,[14] aptly named Orient-Express hotels, trains and cruises back in the early 2000s, was to oversee the setup of the Hiram Bingham train service, on the famous Cusco to Machu Picchu rail tracks. At the time, I was the corporate food and beverage director for the company, in Peru. Together with the corporate executive chef, we were given the responsibility to set up a new luxury catering service onboard the train.

Figure 2.9 *The Hiram Bingham train, luxury travel to Machu Picchu*

The story goes that the owner of Orient-Express hotels had spotted, during one of his many international travels, a set of beautiful and seemingly left-aside carriages, in a Singapore train station. It turns out they had been manufactured in South Africa.

---

[14] Belmond Ltd. (formerly Orient-Express Hotels Ltd.) is a hospitality and leisure company that operates luxury hotels, train services, and river cruises worldwide. www.belmond.com

*Figure 2.10 Hiram Bingham's carriages, manufactured in
South Africa*

A few months later, the owner decided to purchase the carriages
and to have them shipped to Peru, where they undertook a set of necessary transformations: firstly, the wheel gauge of the carriages had
to be adjusted to the width of Peruvian railways, which are narrower.
Extensive renovation work followed, as well as mechanical improvement, and interior design: the result was pure 1920s Pullman style, for
which Orient-Express is known: simply amazing! Peruvian craftsmen
are among the best I have ever worked with. Give them a photo of any
furniture, fixture, or fitting and they will craft it out of any material!

*Figure 2.11 Table setup in the Hiram Bingham restaurant's
carriages*

After many months of fine-tuning details, the train was ready to roll on the railways of its new country of adoption, for countless journeys alongside the fabulous Peruvian Andes, slowly descending, as Machu Picchu is actually at a lower attitude than Cusco, into the deep rainforest.

The journey from Cusco to Machu Picchu is breathtaking and offers a perfect example of *slow luxury tourism*: a 3.5-hour trip for a distance of around 60 miles: which gave us ample time to serve a four-course meal. Great way to enjoy the train ride, enjoying Peruvian gastronomy, a few pisco sours,[15] while sitting down in a comfortable seat and enjoying beautiful scenery. Tour guides are also on the train and accompany the guests during the citadel's visit.

Our food and beverage mission was only beginning: setting up two dining room carriages, a bar and observation carriage, and a fourth carriage dedicated to the kitchen operations. At that time, Peru Rail, the only touristic train operator at the time, partly owned by Orient-Express, was offering train services to and from Machu Picchu, but with very limited catering: sandwiches, soft drinks, and snacks.

After months of refurbishment, our new *working tool*, a food and beverage director and chef's dream, had arrived at the station: two 42-seat carriages, a kitchen carriage, and an observation bar. Our first goal was to create two menus, adapted to life on wheels, which can be quite shaky on Andean rails! Also, the size of the kitchen and availability of products limited our offer to set menus, rather than à la carte, which would have required a much larger kitchen. Many other specific details had to be taken into consideration: the high altitude, the availability of products, the space constraints, and the logistics involved. For example, some of the main kitchen production was assured by the Machu Picchu Sanctuary Lodge, and another part was realized in Cusco. Dishwashing was partly done onboard the train, so chinaware and glassware would not have to be offloaded after every single trip.

---

[15] Pisco sour is an alcoholic cocktail, considered to be the national drink of Peru. It is made with Pisco liquor, a distilled product of white wine, egg white, and sugar.

Other than those specific considerations, setting up the Hiram Bingham train was similar to opening a new restaurant: choice of staff's uniforms, choice of tableware, staff selection and recruitment, training ... and of course menu planning. Follow along, for all of these particular topics will be discussed further throughout the following chapters.

Food and Beverage Trends

This section highlights the current and future trends affecting the food and beverage industry. It is by no means exhaustive, as they are in constant and rapid evolution. Trends vary from country to country, city to city, and are often influenced by societal changes, such as veganism and the environment's protection in the latest years. The aim of this section is to help the reader understand trends' impact on the activities related to food and beverage management and provide recommendations to meet future guests' expectations.

The 2010–2020 decade brought on new societal, environmental, political, and technical forces that have helped shape the current trends. Four main categories emerge, driving the changes taking place in the food and beverage industry:

- Technology
- Social responsibility
- Health
- Menu contents

Technology

Technology is evolving rapidly in all sectors, as we collectively embrace increasingly connected lifestyles around the world. While fully robotized restaurants are not yet common, many technological innovations, which rose during the last decade, are greatly impacting the customer's experience in restaurants.

One illustration of this is the multiplication of online grocery stores, such as *Amazon dash buttons*, and home delivery applications such as Deliveroo or Uber, used by millions of customers daily.[16] These interfaces are shaping the new relationships to come for future food and beverage operators; they increase efficiency by providing faster interactions and allowing greater customization, thus enhancing a customer's experience.

They also act as data collectors, providing restaurant operators with a wealth of information, allowing customers to place an order, anywhere, anytime. "People don't care! It's 'push a button, get food,'" as quoted by Peter Schatzberg, partner and founder of New York's Green Summit group,[17] operator of *virtual restaurants*.

Cashless payments, such as Apple Pay, are becoming the norm, and numerous chains are experimenting electronic fingerprints, retina scans, and facial recognition as the next means of payment. The objective is, once again, to enhance customer experience, gain time, but also to reduce operational issues such as the risk of errors or theft.

Data collection and artificial intelligence are increasingly being used as a means to personalize service, for example, KFC restaurants have introduced license plate scanning at their drive through,[18] in order to recognize repeat guests and offer suggestions based on their previous choices. Voice and facial recognition are also being tested by those companies.

Without surprise, the Covid sanitary crisis has been greatly accelerating these technological trends, converting them almost instantly in the new industry norms. The big winners are undoubtedly the establishments using online ordering and delivery services. On the other hand, restaurants mainly relying on guest presence will have to catch up and quickly adapt to the new contactless norms, in order to stand a chance of surviving in the months ahead.

---

[16] https://forbes.com/sites/sarwantsingh/2019/09/09/the-soon-to-be-200b-online-food-delivery-is-rapidly-changing-the-global-food-industry/#3e3346eb1bcb

[17] https://crainsnewyork.com/article/20160221/HOSPITALITY_TOURISM/160219856/these-ghost-restaurants-could-spell-the-death-of-traditional-restaurant-delivery

[18] https://latimes.com/business/la-fi-license-plate-recognition-drive-through-restaurant-20190711-story.html

Social Responsibility

With the globalization of information, news travels very fast. Therefore, the need for transparency from food and beverage operators has increased tremendously. Customers are no longer just expecting quality at a fair price; there is also a sense of responsibility and purpose in the simple act of consuming food and beverages. Such new ethics in business require operators to go the extra mile to ensure they know and control all aspects of their supply chain from the producer to the distributors and various other intermediaries.

The role of the restaurateur needs to respond to these expectations by being aware of, and bringing together, the interests and needs of customers, employees, suppliers, shareholders, communities, and the planet. Vast program indeed! And, all of this under the constant scrutiny of social networks and evaluation sites such as TripAdvisor, Yelp, or La Fourchette, to name a few.

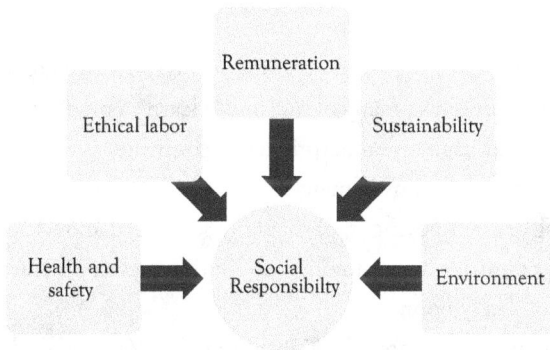

Figure 2.12 Social responsibility

Beyond the obvious benefits of reducing the overall carbon footprint and reducing energy and resource consumption, there are many other reasons why organizations should be more *socially responsible*. For example, research and experience have proven that sustainability significantly improves financial results and helps companies achieve better bottom lines, by reducing operational costs and improving productivity. Other benefits for the company include an enhanced brand image and reputation, an increase in sales and customer loyalty, and an ability to attract and retain employees in a sector that is known for high staff turnover rates and having difficulties in recruiting.

One way to reduce carbon footprint is to favor short food circuits: this has given birth to the *locavorism* trend: locally sourced products, supporting farms and producers from and for the local community. The best example to illustrate this trend is the *Farm to table* movement, which could become, in the no so distant future, *Lab to table* (more in next section *Health*).

> *Luxury hospitality's inside story: Luxury hospitality meeting sustainable tourism at The Sumba hotel school, Sumba Island, Indonesia*

One thing I strongly value in life is to be useful to others in one way or another; after all, that is what the hospitality business is all about: be at the service of others, isn't it? It is also the reason why I chose to work in this field many years ago, alongside my insatiable urge to explore this small world!

In this regard, I have always considered myself fortunate to be able to travel and work in so many places and to learn so much from others. Having worked in many underprivileged countries, I often witnessed how the living conditions of many could be changed through hospitality training and employment, particularly so in Peru and Mexico, both successful countries when it comes to tourism development, but also very economically poor.

So, when I first heard, through the Ecole Hôtelière de Lausanne network, about Sumba Hospitality Foundation,[19] a small but promising hotel school located South of Bali, in Indonesia, on Sumba Island, I contacted their management team to find out how I could help in any way. I was given the opportunity to deliver a two-week course on the basics of wine production and service to their students. The school was founded in July 2016 and is dedicated to educating underprivileged students from the four regions of Sumba Island.

---

[19] www.sumbahospitalityfoundation.org

Figure 2.13 Wine trainees at the Sumba Hospitality School, certificates in hand

Students are able to train in real-life industry conditions. To enable this, five luxury guest rooms were built on site, as well as a bar, a restaurant, and a spa. The facilities are very cleverly designed and are all made in a sustainable way; the construction is entirely made of bamboo. Everything you would expect from a luxury hotel is there: comfortable bedding, wonderful outdoor shower, laundry service, and great onsite-grown organic food served at the restaurant. Furthermore, the Foundation recycles water and produces its own electricity through solar power.

But, what truly sets Sumba Hospitality Foundation apart is the atmosphere felt at the hotel school. Management and teaching staff are genuinely dedicated to their task, which is to help those young Sumbanese students improve their lives through hospitality education. For my part, sharing some of my knowledge with them is an experience I will never forget, and I am grateful I was able to be part of their learning journeys in the rich world of hospitality.

The school is only a few years old, but some of the graduates have already secured jobs in the hospitality industry, in renowned luxury hotels or restaurant, mostly on nearby Bali Island, such as the Nusantara Ubud, one of the best restaurants in town.

Figure 2.14 Nusantara restaurant in Ubud, Bali[20]

The Foundation was recently spotted as one of the best places to experience *voluntourism*, or tourism with a real purpose: help others.[21]

Health

In a 2017 study, 1.6 percent of the global restaurant consumers claimed to be vegan, an increase of 61 percent from 2014. During the same period, the number of vegetarians has been declining from 14 to 5 percent.[22] It is quite obvious that more and more people are moving toward a plant-based lifestyle, for many different reasons, which often combine with one another. For example, the desire to reduce animal suffering combined with the need to reduce greenhouse gas emissions lead many consumers, principally in the younger generations, to favor meatless diets.

Also, as medical research moves forward, more evidence is gathered each day, confirming that we really *are what we eat*. For example, many

---

[20] One of the many establishments offering training sessions to Sumba Hospitality School students.

[21] https://cntraveller.com/gallery/voluntourism-holidays

[22] https://globaldata.com/quorns-investments-vegan-foods-evidence-veganism-successfully-captures-consumers-secondary-dieting-concerns/

studies link health risks, such as cardiovascular diseases or high blood pressure, with the consumption of animal products such as red meat.[23]

The success of websites such as veganuary.com shows that veganism is on the rise, as the millennial generation is increasingly aware of the many ways food consumption affects health, and the environment. A couple of years back, chefs could *get away* with a couple of vegan dishes on the menu. This is no longer the case. Even meat lovers are starting to question their habits, thus reducing their meat consumption, for health reasons but also for environmental purposes: the flexitarian diet is here to stay!

Flexitarians favor hybrid blends of meats and vegetables, to lower the amount of meat consumption, without giving it up altogether. For this reason the food and beverage operator should offer many healthy options on the menu, vegetarian and vegan dishes, and environmentally friendly products.

Plant-based foods are popping up on restaurants menus; products such as kelp algae are becoming the new *super products*. Some restaurants are even experimenting *clean meat*, such as meatballs grown from animal stem cells, without raising and killing any animal. *Beyond Meat* company has recently announced pigs *made* by using such processes: welcome to *Lab to table!*[24] Veganism and the flexitarian diet are also promoting the rise of what is now called *Faux foods*: almond or rice milk, dairy products made of cashew nuts, meatless chicken or foie gras, plant-based burgers such as Burger King's *Impossible Whopper*.[25]

Fast-casual restaurants are adapting to these trends by promoting *lifestyle bowls*: price-set bowls that correspond to the most common diets such as keto, paleo, high protein, or plant based.

Protection of the environment, reduction of animal suffering, fighting against climate change are high on the millenials' list of priorities, but so is health consciousness. This pushes millennials to cut back on alcohol consumption too, and alcohol-free cocktails such as the famous Spritzer are becoming trendy. Biodynamic wines, grown in very specific ways using no chemicals and respecting moon phases, are appearing on wine

---

[23] https://nih.gov/news-events/nih-research-matters/eating-red-meat-daily-triples-heart-disease-related-chemical

[24] https://cnet.com/health/beyond-meats-new-breakfast-sausage-what-it-tastes-like-and-how-it-gets-made/

[25] https://impossiblefoods.com/burgerking/

lists too, responding to the growing environment and health-conscious-ness movement in society.

Menu Contents

Many restaurants now offer multicultural choices in their menus, stepping away from the single-cuisine specialty restaurant concept. There are many examples of cross-cultural fusions such as Mexican and South East Asian, Peruvian Chifa (a combination of Peruvian and Chinese cuisines), or Nikkei (a combination of Peruvian and Japanese cuisines). In Peru, chefs such as Gaston Acurio[26] have been leaders in these trends. His latest restaurant concept, *Madam Tusan*,[27] in Lima, is entirely dedicated to Chifa. For many years, Lima has been home to many Nikkei restaurants, such as the famous Matsuei restaurant, which was opened by internationally acclaimed Japanese chef Nobu[28] in 1973.

Levantine cuisines, from Israel, Turkey, or Lebanon are also becoming increasingly popular. They are often made of many colorful, healthy ingredients and offer many possibilities of table sharing and snacking, rather than formal dining.

Scandinavian cuisine is still booming, most probably because it uses so many natural ingredients, often from the wild or fresh from the sea. It is increasingly being fusioned with French or other European cuisines: a perfect illustration of this is Gård,[29] a small chain of restaurants with presence in European capitals such as Brussels, London, or Amsterdam.

---

[26] Gastón Acurio Jaramillo (born October 30, 1967) is a Peruvian chef and ambassador of Peruvian cuisine. He owns several restaurants throughout multiple countries and is the author of several books. In Peru, he is the host of his own television program and contributes to a few culinary magazines (Wikipedia).

[27] http://madamtusan.pe/

[28] Nobuyuki Nobu Matsuhisa born March 10, 1949, is a Japanese celebrity chef and restaurateur known for his fusion cuisine blending traditional Japanese dishes with Peruvian ingredients. His signature dish is black cod in miso. He has restaurants bearing his name in several countries. He has also played small parts in three major films (Wikipedia).

[29] https://gardtastescandinavian.com/

2020 and Beyond: Preparing the Future

Technological influence will be reinforced in all segments of the food and beverage industry, with an increasing use of artificial intelligence in guest and restaurateur's interactions.

Specific diets such as keto, vegan, flexitarian, gluten-free, dairy free should increase in popularity; the use of alternative ingredients such as almond or rice-based flours, cereal-based milk will increase, with a promotion of local, authentic cuisine.

The decrease in alcohol consumption will continue, giving space for new beverage preparation. Coffee is an example of new beverage preparations: it is being used in many new ways: coffee spritzers, Espresso Tonic, or even CBD coffee.

These societal changes bring about numerous challenges for food and beverage operators, and they will have to adapt rather rapidly in order to survive.

As we are in the midst of Covid-19, many of the future trends presented in this chapter are actually being the norm already today. There is a tremendous *fast forwarding* of technological and nutritional trends taking place in the food and beverage industry today, in order to keep up with the new requirements the crisis imposes on all society. Every effort needs to be considered in order to guarantee health and safety during all stages of food and beverage transactions. As a result, restaurant operators are streamlining their operations to allow increased takeout, deliveries, click and collect, and contactless payment.

Transparency on the products used in the kitchen is also becoming vital, as more and more consumers are looking for healthier ingredients, less processed. For all these reasons, a strong online presence, with a user-friendly website or application, is becoming the new basic requirement for any food and beverage venture.

Here are a few recommendations for food and beverage managers, chefs, or restaurant owners, in order to maximize their chances to stay in the race.

Flexibility

- Adapt operating hours to the restaurant's market

- Customize the dining room, giving the ability to create a variety of atmospheres throughout the day
- Personalize menus and meals: create menus that are easy to personalize and customize, propose different sizes or portions
- Be transparent: indicate allergens, use applications informing the customer of contents, product's origin, ingredients, and so on … and allow customer to save his or her health profile for future ordering or suggestions

Promotion

- Be everywhere all the time: reinforce online presence by creating a website that enables ordering and featuring virtual visits. Be *instagramable*, and frequently update social media contents
- Interact: offer the possibility for customers to upload their nutrition or health profile, reserve specific table. Guest comment and evaluation management, profile management on Facebook, TripAdvisor, La Fourchette, immediate interaction with consumers are the new skills to have for any 2020 restaurateur

Customer experience

- Ease procedures for the customer: payment, reservations, user-friendly interface
- Develop a clear concept, update it frequently by keeping abreast of culinary trends, and so on
- Packaging needs to be adapted for the different dishes delivered, and follow strict Covid-19 hygiene guidelines
- Be environmentally friendly, and make it known to your customers
- Ordering and payment through digital means should be available
- Delivery, takeaway option becomes mandatory, through your own application or website, or by registering with a delivery platform

Transparency

- Highlight the origin of products, the ingredients used, as well as the methods of production
- Promote suppliers and homemade products. Keep sourcing as local as possible, by developing a network of local suppliers: farmers, fishermen, growers, and make sure they are promoted within your business
- Inform on the presence of allergens
- Detail hygiene procedures in all aspects of the operation, in order to keep customers reassured
- Clearly display Covid-19 guidelines and processes, onsite and online

Health

- Provide balanced meals
- Highlight nutritional aspects
- Promote healthy meals
- Provide information on anti-Covid-19 measures at all times

Environment

- Reduce food waste to a minimum, recycle ingredients whenever possible
- Implement recycling policies
- Offer environmentally friendly solutions for packaging, tableware
- Grow your own garden!

CHAPTER 3

The Food and Beverage Department

Keywords				
À la carte	Department	Kitchen	Policies	Silverware
Back of the	Director	Luxury	Prime cost	Sommelier
house	Events	Maintenance	Procedures	Standards
Banqueting	Executive chef	Maître d'hôtel	Production	Station
Bars	Expenses	Management	Profitability	Stock
Brigade	Food and beverage	Menus	Purchasing	Storage
Buffet	director	Michelin	Quality	Supervisor
Catering	Front of the	Mise en place	Recipe	Suppliers
Chef de partie	house	Organizational	Revenue	Tableware
Chef de rang	Glassware	charts	Roster	Teamwork
Chief steward	Head of	Outlet	Runner	Training
Commis	department	Outside	Sales	Waiter
Cuisine	Headwaiter	catering	Section	Wedding
Customers	Hygiene	Par stock	Service styles	
Cutlery	Inventories	Pastry	Shift	
	Job description	Plated		

Objectives of the Food and Beverage Department

If the main objective of the food and beverage department had to be summed up in one sentence, it could be something along these lines:

"The food and beverage department is responsible for maintaining high and consistent quality of food and beverage products and service and for providing sound management of prime cost and other expenses."

The most challenging part of it is that quality is highly subjective. Most customers nowadays are very sensible to the service experience. A great experience may be true for a guest and not perceived as such by another. The same applies to any dish on the menu, which may not suit all tastes.

The two other points, management and cost, are closely linked: successful management will generally lead to effective cost control, and control activities are a great part of management's activities: you cannot manage what you do not measure.

One of the most important aspects of any food and beverage operation is its staffing structure: in most cases, the food and beverage department will represent anywhere between 30 and 50 percent of a hotel's workforce.

In more general terms, the main responsibilities and objectives of a food and beverage department may be listed as follows:

- Provide food and beverage products and services to pre-identified markets, constantly thriving to exceed customers' expectations
- Food and beverage production on the premises for final service to the customer
- Implementation of an efficient overall control system within the department
- Monitoring of menu pricing and dishes' popularity
- Compilation of relevant food and beverage financial information on a weekly, monthly, and annual basis
- Selection, recruitment, training, and motivation of food and beverage staff
- Establish an efficient and timely guest feedback collection system so that collected comments are taken into account to improve service standards

Let us now have a look at the department's structure.

Food and Beverage Departmental Structure

The food and beverage department is divided in two sub-departments, the front of the house (FOH) and the back of the house (BOH):

Front of the house

FOH is made of all personnel having a direct contact with customers: service staff in a restaurant, bartender, room service waiter, restaurant host or hostess, and so on.

Figure 3.1 Food and beverage front of the house staff

Back of the house

The food and beverage BOH is made up of two main sections: the kitchen and stewarding department. The kitchen is responsible for the production of food in the various food and beverage outlets, while stewarding takes care of the less-glamorous side of the business, but nonetheless extremely important: hygiene and cleanliness of kitchens. Another key role attributed to stewarding is tableware management.

Figure 3.2 Kitchen department

In the next section, different organizational charts are presented. Organizational charts vary, depending on the size of the hotel, and the management structure of the food and beverage operations.

Organizational Charts

Classical fine-dining restaurant, based on the French brigade

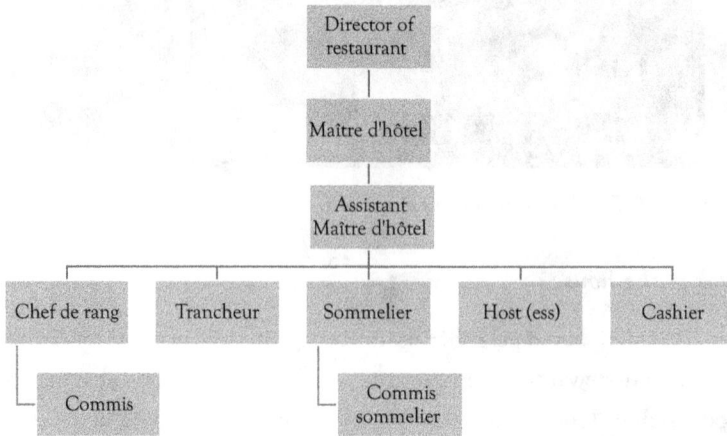

Figure 3.3 Classical fine-dining restaurant organizational chart

Food and beverage organization in a small-size hotel

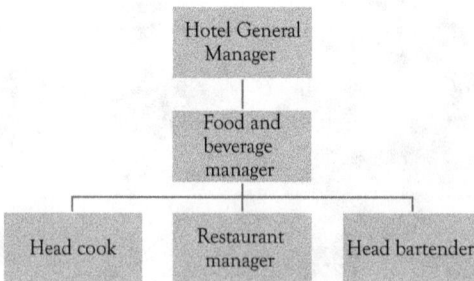

Figure 3.4 Small-size hotel organizational chart

Food and beverage organization in a medium-sized hotel

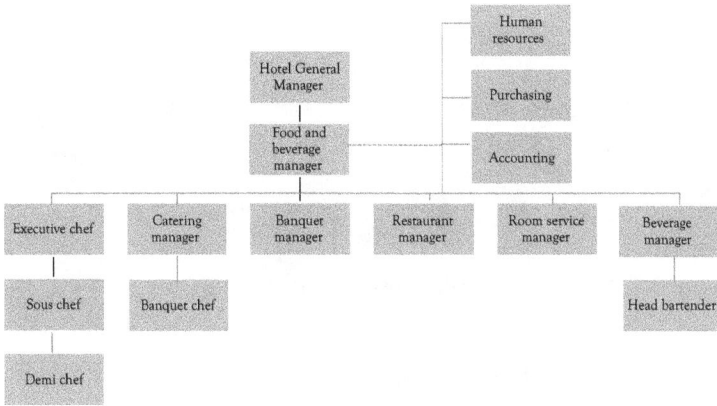

Figure 3.5 Medium-sized hotel organizational chart

Food and beverage organization in a large hotel

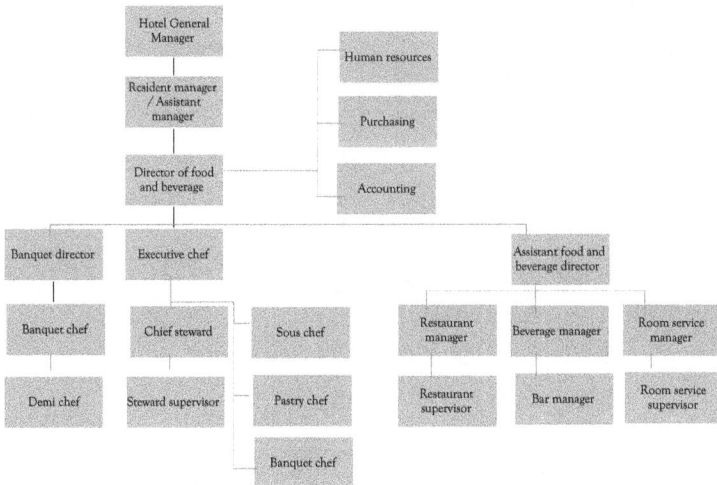

Figure 3.6 Large hotel organizational chart

Small, independent restaurant structure

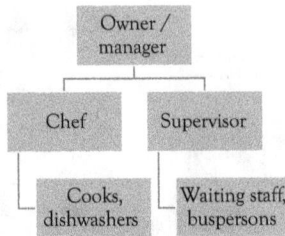

Figure 3.7 Small, independent restaurant structure

Front of the House Staff

Keywords	
Food and beverage manager	**Commis**
Outlet manager	**Runner**
Maître d'hôtel	**Sommelier**
Supervisor	**Bartender**
Headwaiter	**Lounge staff**
Station waiter	**Banqueting staff**
Waiter	

While there have been many changes in food and beverage service organizations, four key requirements remain for all FOH staff:

- Sound product knowledge
- Competent technical skills
- Well-developed social skills
- Ability to work as part of a team

The required set of skills greatly vary from restaurant to restaurant: for example, a Michelin-starred restaurant will require very precise technical skills such as carving or executing complex recipes, which can only be acquired after years of training in the field. On the other hand, a fast-food outlet will require organizational skills and methods of production, which are highly standardized and may be acquired in a few weeks' training.

The type of service in a Michelin-starred restaurant also determines which technical and social skills are required: the interaction with the guest needs to be highly tailored to his or her perceived expectations, and therefore cannot be *taught* in a manual in a few weeks. Another example to illustrate this is the sommelier's knowledge of the wine list, which is a determinant for a successful guest experience.

Having said that, any type of restaurant shares common foundations, regardless of the number of stars or the category it evolves in: high standards of personal grooming and hygiene, integrity, honesty, respect of others, and professionalism.

In the following section, we look at the key positions found in the FOH.

The Food and Beverage Manager or Director

Mainly responsible for the efficient and effective operation of:

- Any food and beverage outlets, such as restaurants, room service, minibars, lounges and bars
- Banqueting, catering, special events, external contracted services
- Kitchen and stewarding, jointly with the executive chef

Note that the term manager or director may be employed to designate a similar position. Generally speaking, a director's title will be in use in larger establishments, where the role will take on a more strategic approach, rather than operational. In this particular situation, a food and beverage manager may act as the director's *assistant* or *number two*. The food and beverage manager or director is the ship's captain when it comes to food and beverage. He or she will usually report to the hotel manager or the general manager.

Depending on the size of the establishment, the food and beverage manager or director is either in charge of implementing agreed policies or for contributing to the setting of food and beverage policies. The larger the organization, the less likely the food and beverage manager or director is to be involved in policy setting. In large operations, there may be a food and beverage director, and one or various food and beverage managers reporting to him, depending on the scope of responsibilities and the number of outlets.

In general, food and beverage managers or directors are responsible for:

- Ensuring required profit margins are achieved for each food and beverage service area, during each financial period
- Updating and compiling new wine lists according to availability of stock, current trends, and customer expectations
- Compiling, in liaison with the kitchen, menus for the various food service areas and for special occasions
- Coordinating purchases of all materials, equipment, food and drink, with the support from the purchasing department
- Ensuring that the quality in relation to the price paid is maintained
- Determining the portion size in relation to selling price, in coordination with the executive chef
- Ensuring staff training takes place as planned with the human resources department
- Planning and marketing food and beverage culinary promotions

In many cases, the executive chef will report to the food and beverage manager or director. In medium to large operations, a food and beverage assistant manager may also assist the head of department.

Luxury hospitality's inside story: a day in life as corporate food and beverage director for Belmond Hotels Peru

The Hotel Monasterio, located in Cusco, Peru, and flagship of Belmond hotels in the country, hosted our corporate base for food and beverage operations. Both the corporate executive chef and I were responsible for the smooth day-to-day running of four hotels: the previously named Hotel Monasterio, the Machu Picchu Sanctuary Lodge, the Miraflores hotel in Lima, and the Parador del Colca in the South of Peru, close to Arequipa. In addition to this, as described in Chapter 2, the catering operations on the Hiram Bingham's train were also under our responsibility.

All in all, that meant we kept busy overseeing 10 restaurants, room service operations in each of the hotels, as well as banqueting, outside catering, and bars. The combined food and beverage teams, made of the FOH and BOH, represented on average 350 employees.

The main purpose of any hotel management expatriate in a foreign country is to develop future local managers, which will take over after you have left on to another country, usually two or three years later. It starts with identifying the most suitable candidates, in order to develop them as the next generation of leaders.

Being in charge of multiple outlets in various locations around the country requires faultless organization and an ability to delegate tasks, and empower managers, giving them adequate levels of independence to run their departments, and regularly report on results. I found out that the most effective way to achieve this is to surround yourself well: during my first few months of observation in the Cusco, Lima, and Machu Picchu hotels, I was able to identify many internal talents.

Some of them rose the ranks quite quickly and soon became local food and beverage managers, in the various hotels, and on the Hiram Bingham train when it started operating. Most of them had started as trainees in the various hotels, and in a couple of years, they had become promising young food and beverage managers. As far as I am aware, most of them still remain working for Belmond Hotels today.

Management technical skills are one thing; another important point is to find the right fit for a certain position: for example, the banqueting and conference manager in Miraflores Hotel in Lima was a local resident, very much aware of who is who in the city, with an ability to draw business to the hotel, in the form of social events such as weddings and outside catering. Despite the fact she did not have a formal hotel management education, she exceled in this role, as she generated a great amount of trust toward potential clients.

The chef is a key element of the food and beverage management team, and close collaboration with him proved very helpful when managing multiple properties: a relationship based on trust was established from the start, and we supported each other in all aspects of the operation, for example, by ensuring we would not always travel to the same locations at the same time. That way, we would keep a broader view on the different operations simultaneously. Careful planning of the journeys to the various locations was essential: even with the best empowered managers, management cannot be performed at a distance. Also, high-profile and very important events, such as the Cumbre de Rio (see Chapter 3, customer service and crisis management), require visibility and support from senior management.

With managers in place in all the strategic locations, operations in Peru were generally running smoothly, and guest satisfaction levels usually quite high. This is mostly because of Peruvians being a naturally hospitable people. Most of the employees went out of their ways to ensure customers were having great experiences in the hotels and train. The teams even scored the best Leading Hotels of the World scores during mystery guests' inspections that took place twice a year.

Having this fairly under control, I was able to dedicate a fair amount of time to the department's strategic growth: determining and updating financial targets, marketing and food and beverage policies, and roll out main objectives for the department. There were also many ongoing development projects that required a great deal of attention, such as the Hiram Bingham train conversion into a restaurant on wheels (see Chapter 2, Andean meals on wheels: setting up Hiram Bingham's luxury catering service).

On any given month, I would spend most of my time at Hotel Monasterio and schedule a week in Lima's hotel, making it coincide with specific events that were to take place or a special food and beverage promotion in a restaurant. Visits to Machu Picchu took place once or twice monthly, and I would of course take the opportunity to travel there on the Hiram Bingham train.

This allowed me follow-up on any pending requirements and assist the team onboard and check that service standards were being followed. As a general rule, it is necessary to try and keep track of each member of staff, no matter the size of the team, so that no one feels forgotten and starts to feel demotivated in their work. The Hiram Bingham staff started their day very early in the morning and went straight to the train station, and they came back late at night, so traveling on the train was a good way to keep communication running between management and employees.

My day at Hotel Monasterio would start quite early, usually around 7.30 a.m., to make sure breakfast service was starting on the right foot, and that the buffet was fully stocked and looking presentable. I would also take time to check on staff grooming and overall cleanliness of the restaurant and BOH.

The hotel had 126 rooms, and most of the guests were familiar faces after a day stay. I spent some time in the dining room greeting them and making sure they were having a great stay. When breakfast service slowed down, I would sit at the back of the restaurant to have a light breakfast with a strong cup of coffee, another opportunity to check on the quality standards in food and beverage.

Morning time was dedicated to liaising with the chef on the upcoming day's operations and getting activities in motion: preparation of events, organization of meetings, administrative work, e-mails. Our teamwork was made easier as we shared the same office, together with the assistant food and beverage manager.

Daily briefings were held with the hotel management team at 10 a.m., in those meetings were discussed any complaints or issues from the day before, details on VIP (very important persons) arrivals, special events, follow-up on maintenance work, or any other relevant matters. The briefing was chaired by the general manager, or by myself during his absence, as my role was also to fill in when he was away on business trips or on holidays.

Right after that briefing, which lasted 15 minutes on average, it was time for our food and beverage daily meeting, where all outlet managers, or their assistants, gave a brief outlook on the previous day's operations, report on sales revenue, and number of covers. The second part of the meeting was about the current day's operations. The chef would also be present and highlight any relevant information from the kitchen: any missing ingredients, special dishes of the day, events, outside catering, maintenance requests, and so on.

By the time it was over, it was time for the teams to get ready for lunch service in the outlets. Lunchtime was one of the day's peak time, as we were often fully booked with outside groups coming to enjoy the Monasterio's cuisine at restaurant Illariy. The hotel, at the time, was the only place in town where a five-star experience could be had, for both food and service, the reputation it enjoyed was excellent.

As for breakfast service, I would check on quality standards such as grooming, guest welcome, but also the temperature and presentation of dishes as they came out from the kitchen pass. Speed of service was important too, as most guests were on a tight timetable, with many activities programmed in the afternoon. Nevertheless, I would also make a point of stopping by each table to make sure each and every customer was fully satisfied with the meal and service.

The afternoon was the perfect time for longer meetings, such as the ones organized in preparation of large functions or special events or strategic meetings with other departments. It could be, for example, the finance department, for a review of last month's profit and loss statement, or the sales and marketing department, when preparing a food and beverage promotion in one of the food and beverage outlets. These few hours were also necessary for long-term planning activities, such as budgeting for the food and beverage department, or staff-related matters, such as recruitment, promotions, or yearly evaluations.

Analyzing food and beverage results and reporting back to our corporate headquarters in Lima was also an ongoing activity; from these various analysis, action plans would be drafted, and a list of corresponding objectives for improvement would be defined.

Evening service was also very important, as the Illariy restaurant was usually fully booked, this time with in-house guests returning from their visits to Machu Picchu or other historical sites nearby. The restaurant's atmosphere was entirely different from lunch time, as night time came on quite early. Its setup also was distinct, as we used white cotton linen, and the à la carte offer was different from the lunch one.

Dinner service was also a great opportunity to have longer interactions with guests while they were enjoying their meals, without having to worry about the train or tour bus leaving them behind!

Whenever we catered for special events, or if the restaurant was very crowded, I would stay until the end of service, to make sure service went smoothly and without any unresolved complaints. On slower nights, I allowed myself to leave the restaurant earlier, to follow-up on administrative work or simply get a little rest home! Being in this strategic position, there are no predetermined schedules, one must act as an entrepreneur in charge of his or her own business and decide when to be in the restaurant and when it is fine to leave.

On any day, I would spend an average of 70 percent of my time in the outlets, interacting as much as possible with the guests and the staff, and the rest of the time left would be for strategic planning, administrative work, and meetings.

There is always something to do and something new to learn, as I always say, the main difficulty sometimes in this occupation is that it is highly addictive, and if you are not careful, you could end up spending your whole life in the hotel, which is not the objective! So, work and life balance needs to be monitored carefully too.

Figure 3.8 The five-star Hotel Monasterio in Cusco, Peru

Job Description

SECTION ONE	JOB OUTLINE

Job Title	Dept.
Food and beverage manager	Food and beverage

Division	Job Code	Job Level
Food and beverage service	Manager	3

Reports Directly to:
Executive assistant manager – Food and beverage

Supervises:
Waiters/Waitress/Supervisors/assistant outlet manager/Outlet manager/assistant food and beverage manager

Other Relationships:
All departments of the hotel
Customers / Suppliers

Job Summary/Purpose: To supervise and control all catering outlets in a hotel to the required standards, within agreed budgetary limits and parameters of the law.

Key Areas: Responsible for all restaurant, room service, banqueting, stores, and back of the house staff. (In some cases, the head chef will also report to the food and beverage manager.)

SECTION TWO	KEY AREAS

Job Title	Food and beverage manager

Duties and Responsibilities:
1. Attitude
To reflect the hotel's philosophy by providing highest quality of friendly service to our customer. He or she is to lead by example, always adopting a positive attitude to keep team spirit at its highest.
To greet with smile all the time colleagues or guests anywhere in the hotel (front or back of the house).
To have pride in his or her appearance and personal hygiene, making sure that his or her uniform and shoes are always of the highest standards.
To remain confidential about all matters of such nature.
2. Responsibilities
To ensure the prompt and efficient service of all meals, snacks, functions, and beverages to the required standards.

Figure 3.9 Food and beverage manager's job description

To ensure that profit margins are maintained, agreed costs are not exceeded through effective control systems, including issuing against dockets, sales analysis, menu costing, and cash checks.

To ensure that restaurants and cloakrooms are clean and well maintained. That table appointments, including flower arrangements, are impeccable.

To ensure that waiters and waitresses are correctly and smartly dressed, that they offer professional and courteous service to their customers.

To ensure that bars and cloakrooms are clean and stocked with stipulated requirements.

To ensure that bar personnel are well trained, correctly and smartly dressed, and serve their customers in a professional and friendly manner.

To ensure that room service orders are executed promptly, and that they comply with the required standards.

To ensure that room service staff is correctly and smartly dressed and serve customers in a professional and friendly manner.

To ensure the efficient running of the banqueting department, and that all banqueting rooms, including cloakrooms, are clean and tidy.

To act as duty manager as required.

To ensure that consumable and non-consumable goods are ordered, correctly stored, and issued to the various departments.

To ensure maximum security in all areas under your control and the staff is fully aware of the importance of key security.

To ensure that staffing levels are correct and to agreed standards and are not exceeded without prior consultation.

To ensure that company and statutory hygiene standards are maintained in all areas.

To attend timeously to customer complaints.

To take the necessary steps in the event of theft, burglary, or fire.

To ensure that reports and administration requirements are timeously submitted.

To ensure that the back of the house department operates effectively and efficiently.

To hold regular performance appraisals with all management staff, identifying areas for development and training needs, and ensuring that this training is effective.

To ensure that the causes of staff grievances are investigated and appropriate action(s) taken.

To ensure that fire and evacuation drills are held regularly.

To ensure that bands and musicians are available when required.

To be fully conversant with all statutory requirements regarding a food and beverage operation. That all licenses, including special licenses, are timeously applied for, and that the conditions affecting the issues of a liquor license are not jeopardized.

To ensure that regular stock takes are conducted.

To prepare and submit on the required format all information necessary for budgeting purposes, timeously and accurately.

To ensure that an effective table reservation system is in operation.

To circulate throughout all restaurants, bars, and banqueting departments, maintaining a high profile with customers and staff.

To hold regular staff meetings.

Figure 3.9 (Continued)

To be fully aware of trends in the industry and make suggestions for improvement of the catering operation.
To attend meetings as required.
To carry out or ensure that regular on-the-job training is taking place to agreed standards.
To ensure that the most suitably qualified person is appointed in the event of a vacancy. Wherever possible, this should be an internal promotion.

SECTION THREE	PERSON SPECIFICATION
Job Title	**Food and beverage manager**
QUALIFICATIONS/ TRAINING	Hygiene training Service oriented trainings Computer literate (Word and Excel)
WORK EXPERIENCE	Minimum of 3 years relevant experience in a 5* hotel, and minimum 7 years in this industry
DISPOSITION Leadership, relationships, character, potential	Ability to work under pressure Excellent people skills, hardworking, and disciplined

Figure 3.9 (Continued)

Outlet Manager

The outlet manager oversees one or several outlets within the food and beverage department. One or several assistants may assist the manager, depending on the outlet's size.

The restaurant manager has the overall responsibility for the organization and administration of particular food and beverage service areas. These may include the lounges, room service (in hotels), restaurants, and possibly some of the private function suites.

It is the outlet manager who sets the standards for service and is responsible for any staff training that may be required, either on or off the job. The outlet manager may compile duty rotas, or rosters holiday lists, and schedule staff's hours on and off duty. He or she will also contribute to operational duties (depending on the size of the establishment) so that all the service areas run efficiently and smoothly.

Maître d'Hôtel

Maître d'hôtel, or Maître d'h., which is a term inherited from the French brigade, are most likely be found in a fine-dining environment, as opposed to the outlet manager. In smaller-sized establishments, the Maître d'hôtel may have the overall responsibility of managing the restaurant. In larger operations, the Maître d'hôtel may act as an assistant outlet manager, or supervisor.

Technically speaking, both the outlet manager and Maître d'hôtel are responsible for the overall outlet operation, although the former is often also in charge of end of the month financial results.

Host, Hostess, Reception Headwaiter or Headwaitress

The host or hostess is responsible for accepting any bookings and for keeping the booking diary up to date. Reservations will then be allocated to particular stations. The host or hostess greets guests on arrival, escorts them to the table, and provides assistance in seating them.

Supervisor/Captain

An outlet supervisor usually will oversee a section of the restaurant. In certain operations, the term *captain* may also be used. The supervisor may also be responsible for a particular shift, for example, the breakfast or dinner service, the night shift for room service or stewarding. The supervisor has the overall charge of the service team and is responsible for seeing that all the pre-preparation duties necessary for service are efficiently carried out, and that nothing is forgotten.

The supervisor will assist Maître d'hôtel during the service and may also take guest orders. He or she also helps with the compilation of duty rosters or schedules, holiday lists, and may relieve the restaurant manager or assistant manager on their off days.

Station Headwaiter or Headwaitress or Section Supervisor

For optimal organization, restaurants are often broken down into sections. The station headwaiter or headwaitress has the overall responsibility for the staff within their station. Each station may represent anything from four to eight tables. The station headwaiter or headwaitress must have excellent knowledge of food and wine, and its service, and be able to instruct and coordinate other members of the staff.

Station Waiter or Waitress or Chef de Rang

The station waiter or waitress provides service to one set of tables, which represents between four and eight tables, and described as a station within the restaurant area. A chef de rang holds similar responsibilities, although the term is usually associated with fine-dining restaurants.

The chef de rang will make sure the table's mise en place has been setup by the waiter or waitress, according to the guest's order, and before dishes are served. They also ascertain guest satisfaction and resolve any potential complaints.

Assistant Station Waiter or Waitress or Demi-Chef de Rang

The assistant station waiter or waitress, or demi-chef de rang, is the person next in seniority to the station waiter or waitress and assists as directed by the station waiter or waitress. They will take over chef de rang's responsibilities whenever it is necessary, for example, when guest counts increase in the station.

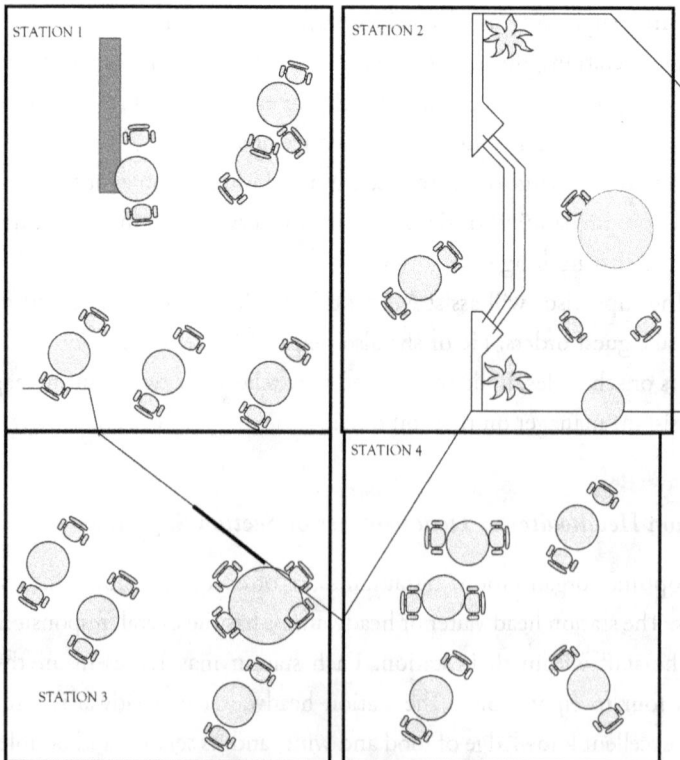

Figure 3.10 Table stations in the restaurant

Waiter or Waitress or Server

The waiter, waitress, or server acts by instruction from the chef de rang. Wait staff mainly fetch and carry dishes from the kitchen to the dining area and may also perform the service of vegetables or sauces. Bread, water service are duties also performed by a waiter or waitress. According to the guest order, they will place the corresponding tableware on the table, for example, a set of fish cutlery for a dish containing a fillet of fish. They also help to clear the tables after each course.

Waiters and waitresses are in direct contact with restaurant guests; for this reason, they are also instrumental in relaying customer feedback to the chef de rang, who will act accordingly.

In fine-dining operations, a waiter or waitress will attend two to four guests at a time, while a fast-casual or a coffee shop operation will require a waiter or waitress to attend 20 to 30 customers simultaneously. In a three-star Michelin restaurant, a waiter or waitress would interact with two or three tables at most during one service.

Wait staff duties include making sure service is carried out smoothly at all times, with great attention to details. Menu knowledge is very important in this position, as the waiter or waitress should be able to answer any menu-related questions and also to increase sales by using upselling techniques.

Commis de Rang

The term *commis* is a French term, inherited from the kitchen brigade, which is used in the kitchen as well. The commis de rang helps the waiter or waitress with the *mise en place*, or table setup according to the guest's menu choices.

During the pre-preparation period, much of the cleaning and pre-paratory tasks will be carried out by the commis de rang. After service, cleaning of the restaurant and equipment preparation for the next service will be the commis' responsibility.

Runner or Bus Person

A *runner*, sometimes called *bus person*, has similar functions to those of a commis de rang. It is a term mostly used in the United States, to describe the service staff that constantly goes to and from the kitchen to the restaurant carrying plates and tableware after cleaning tables.

They may also assist the waiters and waitresses in performing guest service, by bringing dishes from the kitchen into the dining room; however, they usually will not take part in guest service, except if help is required by the commis or waiters or waitresses.

Most of the times, trainees or apprentices, having just joined the food and beverage service staff, will start as runners. During service, the runner will also keep the side station well stocked with equipment and make sure no soiled items are left in the proximity of guest tables.

Sommelier

The sommelier is a wine and beverage specialist, whose main task is to select, and sometimes purchase, in collaboration with the purchasing department, wines and beverages for the establishment. The sommelier also has a fundamental role in ensuring that the wines are correctly stored.

During restaurant service, the sommelier will increase wine sales through customer's advising. The sommelier will also be involved in the creation of wine lists and wine promotions.

Figure 3.11 Sommelier at La Tour d'Argent restaurant, Paris[1]

---

[1] https://tourdargent.com/en/the-wine-cellar/

This is a position typically found in luxury and fine-dining establishments: all palaces or starred Michelin restaurants will have a sommelier on the food and beverage team. Prestigious sommeliers often have many years of experience in luxury environments. Wine is a vast topic, and acquiring knowledge is an ongoing preoccupation of any professional sommelier.

Bartender

As the name suggests, the bartender works behind the bar, which can be an independent outlet or a dispense bar. The position's main responsibilities are drink service, cocktail realization, and keeping an optimal stock of beverages for the operation.

Similar to sommeliers, certain bartenders specialized in luxury establishments will be required to have years of experience in order to develop extensive product knowledge of international beverages.

Lounge Staff

Luxury hotels will offer their guests access to a staffed lobby with drink service. The lounge staff's main duties are to welcome guests and offer warm and cold drink service, as well as a selection of light snacks and pastries. In smaller hotels, it is usually members of the food service staff who will take over these duties as per a pre-established schedule.

The lounge personal may also be responsible for the service of morning coffee, afternoon teas, aperitifs, and liqueurs before and after both lunch and dinner, and any after-meal drinks. Their main duty prior to service is to set up the lounge in the morning and to maintain cleanliness and presentation standards throughout the day.

Banqueting Staff

Banquet service is mainly associated with larger hotels and is not often found in resort hotels, with the exception of those catering to conferences. The hierarchy of positions is similar than that of a restaurant, with a banqueting manager overseeing the department, assisted by one or several assistants, depending on the department's size. The service staff team is usually made of casual or part-time waiters or waitresses, who are solicited on a per-event basis.

> *Luxury hospitality's inside story: banqueting and special events' success rely on highly efficient organizational skills*

A few weeks after starting to work for Orient-Express Hotels, currently Belmond Hotels, in Peru, a small executive committee was formed at the Hotel Monasterio: the advance team liaison committee, in charge of organizing the 17th Cumbre de Rio, featuring heads of states' meetings and conferences from 19 Latin American countries. The main themes that would be discussed and lead to various agreements between the countries' representants were the eradication of poverty, unfortunately always a priority in this part of the world, security in Mexico or Colombia were also high on the Rio Group's agenda.

As the day of the series of gathering, May 23, 2003, was approaching, the group grew larger and larger, involving most of the senior management of the Cusco, Lima, and Machu Picchu hotels. A series of preparation meetings took place during a year, in order to effectively prepare the presidential summits that were to take place in the country.

The *Grupo do Rio*, Rio Group, was created in Rio de Janeiro, on the December 18, 1986. It served as an international organization of Latin American and some Caribbean states. Its founding members were Argentina, Brazil, Colombia, Mexico, Panama, Peru, Uruguay, and Venezuela. It was succeeded in 2011 by the Community of Latin American and Caribbean States.[2]

Unlike the European Union or other multistate organization, the Rio Group did not have a secretariat or permanent body, so its continuity relied on yearly summits of heads of states. So, in 2003, Peru was to host the *XVII Cumbre del Grupo de Río*, and the Hotel Monasterio in Cusco had been chosen to host this prestigious event: we were getting ready to welcome 19 heads of states: leaders of the Republics of Peru, Costa Rica, Argentina, Colombia, Equator, Guatemala, Honduras,

---

[2] https://en.wikipedia.org/wiki/Rio_Group

Nicaragua, Paraguay, Uruguay, Brazil, Bolivia, Chile, El Salvador, Guyana, Panama, Dominica, Venezuela and the Federal Republic of Mexico. CARICOM,[3] representing the Caribbean States, was also invited to the gatherings.

Figure 3.12 Presidents posing for the official picture in Cusco's Hotel Monasterio

Preparing any official state visit, for even *just* one president or minister requires an enormous amount of time, patience, diplomacy, and most of all, flexibility, as there are many last-minute changes, often for security reasons. Coordinating this type of event for 19 presidents, with their respective delegations is a task that took our management teams and the various government representants over a year of intensive preparation work.

---

[3] The Caribbean Community (CARICOM or CC) is an organization of 15 nations and dependencies throughout the Caribbean having primary objectives to promote economic integration and cooperation among its members, to ensure that the benefits of integration are equitably shared, and to coordinate foreign policy. The organization was established in 1973 (Wikipedia).

Well worth it, as everything came out smoothly, and the repercussions for the hotels' image was tremendous. But, it was a bit like preparing a very special dish in a three-star Michelin restaurant: many hours of preparation for a few moments of great intensity.

As for any important guest, many specific requirements had to be met by the hotels. Often, topping the list are food and beverage preferences; in this regard, I will never forget President Hugo Chavez's breakfasts, made of several trays delivered by the room service team every morning! The then President of Venezuela required his own chef to be present in our kitchen to personally supervise the cooking of bacon and eggs and accompanied our room service staff to his presidential suite for any food deliveries. Many other specific constraints had to be taken into account, such as transportation, flight schedules, logistics, press access, and, most importantly, security at all times.

Figure 3.13 Hugo Chavez, the then President of Venezuela

Our main interlocutors were secretaries from the Ministry of Foreign Affairs in Lima, we organized regular meetings at Hotel Monasterio, to get acquainted with the most intricate details of the organization of events that were to take place in the hotels, and in nearby sites such as Sacsayhuaman Archeological Site,[4] the MAP Museum,[5] the Convento de la Merced,[6] and Koricancha Temple.[7]

Figure 3.14 The Inca site of Sacsayhuaman, North of the city of Cusco, Peru

Cusco had never, in its long history, seen such a gathering, and the Peruvian chief of police decided to send an extra 2,000 policemen from the city of Lima, in order to secure the airport and the city. Each presidential convoy would also be surrounded by an impressive number of guards, snipers, bomb squad members.

Needless to say, most Cusco's hotels enjoyed a very healthy occupancy before, during, and after the Cumbre De Rio's events. The events

---

[4] Saqsaywaman, which can be spelled many different ways (possibly from Quechua language, waman falcon or variable hawk), is a citadel on the northern outskirts of the city of Cusco, Peru, the historic capital of the Inca Empire. Sections were first built about 1100 CE by the Killke culture, which had occupied the area since 900 CE (Wikipedia).

[5] The Museum of Precolombian Art in Cusco. https://mapcusco.pe/en/

[6] The Basilica of La Merced, also known as Convent of La Merced, is a minor basilica located in the city of Cusco, Peru. It is located 100 meters southwest of the Plaza de Armas (city's main square) in front of the Plazoleta Espinar. It belongs to the Order of the Blessed Virgin Mary of Mercy and has annexes, both the convent and the premises of La Merced College (Wikipedia).

[7] Coricancha, Koricancha, Qoricancha, or Qorikancha (The Golden Temple, from Quechua quri gold; kancha enclosure) was the most important temple in the Inca Empire. It is located in Cusco, Peru, which was the capital of the empire (Wikipedia).

also helped putting Cusco on the world map and fueled a growth in internal tourism for years to come.

Figure 3.15 One of the Cumbre de Rio's event held in the Convent of La Merced and catered by Hotel Monasterio

JOB DESCRIPTION

SECTION ONE JOB OUTLINE		
Job Title **Banqueting manager**	**Dept.** **Food and beverage**	
Division **Food and beverage** **service**	**Job Code** **Manager**	**Job Level** **5**

Reports Directly to: **Food and beverage manager**
Supervises: Assistant Banqueting manager/Banqueting Coordinator/Banqueting Waiters or waitresses/Stewards
Other Relationships:
Job Summary/Purpose: To supervise and control the banqueting department to the required standards and within agreed budgetary limits. The banquet manager is responsible for the operation, management, and overall performances of the banquet operations. As such, he or she will be directly involved in the day-to-day running of these areas in connecting with staffing, customer service, and product quality. Delegation of duties and responsibilities to his or her assistant manager is necessary to

Figure 3.16 Banquet manager's job description

ensure the proper functioning of all phases of food and beverage service in area under his or her control. He or she is to implement all standardized procedures, rules, and regulations systematically to be in line with hotel standards and policies. It should be noted that the banquet manager can be designated in charge of any area at any time and therefore must have a full and comprehensive working knowledge of all areas within the food and beverage division.

Key Areas:
Attitude
Responsibilities
Guest relation
Sales and revenue
Cost control
Communication
Standard of performance

SECTION TWO	KEY AREAS

Job Title	Banqueting manager

1. Attitude

To reflect the hotel's philosophy by providing highest quality of friendly service to our customers. He or she is to lead by example, always adopting a positive attitude to keep team spirit at its highest.

To greet with smile all the time colleagues or guests anywhere in the hotel (front or back of the house).

To have pride in his or her appearance and personal hygiene, making sure that his or her uniform and shoes are always of the highest standards.

To remain confidential about all matters of such nature.

2. Responsibilities

To ensure that the agreed budgeted targets are achieved or bettered.

To ensure that the food and liquor costs are maintained at their agreed levels, and that the correct profit margins are achieved.

To ensure a prompt, courteous response and follow-up to all enquiries.

To ensure that once a booking is confirmed, all details and requirements are noted, using a checklist, so that nothing is forgotten, for example:

    a. Number of covers
    b. Where to assemble
    c. Where to serve
    d. Details of menu
    e. Plan of tables
    f. Lists of guests
    g. Entertainment

To liaise or ensure liaison with the client a few days before the function to confirm exact numbers, in turn informing the appropriate departmental heads.

Figure 3.16 (Continued)

To ensure that bands or entertainment has been booked as directed.

To ensure that duty rosters are compiled, making certain that adequate numbers of experienced permanent and casual waiting staff will be on duty.

To check the function room, ante rooms, and cloakrooms for cleanliness before guests arrive, table layout and stipulated specific requirements to enable shortcomings to be rectified.

To greet the host and circulate during the course of the function to ensure availability in the event of a problem or complaint.

To ensure that the accounts department receives accurate information to enable it to correctly bill the client.

To ensure that all staff is correctly and smartly dressed at all times.

To ensure effective briefing of waiting staff before the function commences.

To ensure that bar and waiting staff know the limit of open bars and that this is not exceeded.

To ensure that the service food and drink is courteous and professional.

To ensure that tables are correctly set, and that table appointments, including flower arrangements, are impeccable.

To ensure that surplus equipment is removed once the function is over and returned to its correct storage place.

To check equipment against the function checklist to ensure that no items have been misappropriated or mislaid.

To check equipment regularly against the inventory to ensure minimum losses.

To ensure maximum security of all areas under your control, paying particular attention to valuable assets, for example, silverware.

To ensure that all items are used for their correct purpose and not abused, for example, knives used as screwdrivers, tablecloths, or napkins used for cleaning.

To give feedback on guest letters and comments.

To ensure that attendance registers are completed daily in accordance with statutory procedures, and that any anomalies are reported to the personnel department.

To carry out or ensure that regular on-the-job training is carried out to enable staff to perform their duties correctly.

To prepare and submit on the required format all information necessary for budgeting purposes, timeously and accurately.

3. Guest Relation

To promote good relationship with regular guests. To handle any guest's complaint effectively and diplomatically.

4. Sales and Revenue

To maximize sales and revenues by providing excellent service and training staff to upsell.

To capitalize on activities in the hotel and in the community, holidays, and event that would bring in extra customers.

To introduce gimmicks and promotions to the food and beverage director/assistant food and beverage manager to increase sales.

Figure 3.16 (Continued)

5. Cost Control

To control the food and beverage cost of the outlet by implementing strict portion control to prevent any wastage or pilferage. To control the labor cost by proper sales forecasting and scheduling to minimize wastage of manpower.

To ensure that all furniture, equipment, utensils and silverware under his or her charge are accounted for, properly handled, regularly serviced and maintained to prevent excessive wear and tear.

6. Communication

To attend the daily food and beverage morning briefing.

To attend monthly food and beverage and service meetings.

To conduct daily briefing to ensure that all information is adequately shared.

To maintain a logbook for his or her assistant or captain.

To be responsible for a daily report in the form of logbook compiled for all shifts.

To post all current information and standing instructions on the bulletin board.

To write down all food items not available, or seasonal food available on the board for staff's reference.

To communicate and present a positive attitude, and to provide leadership to all staff at all times, in order to attain desired goals.

7. Standard of Performance

Training session to be carried out on a weekly basis with assistant and supervisor.

To ensure that daily training is carried out for all rank and file staff.

Standard checklist for orientation program of staff.

Training program for individual jobs.

Re-train once every three months.

To maintain checklist for daily inspection.

To have a supervisor meeting at least twice a week.

He or she is employed in the food and beverage department, and as such, he or she may be assigned to any area that the management deems suitable and necessary.

Figure 3.16 (Continued)

Back of the House Staff

The kitchen brigade

Keywords	
Executive chef	Commis
Head chef	Pastry chef
Sous chef	Chief baker
Chef de partie	Chef garde manger

Legendary chef Auguste Escoffier (1846–1935), author of the *Le guide culinaire*,[8] and executive chef of the Ritz hotel in Paris is considered to be the inventor of the *Brigade de Cuisine*.[9]

The concept of brigade is derived from a military-type organization, highly structured and aiming to rationalize the various tasks of production. This concept is still largely used in the modern kitchen today, composed of the different sections, which will be developed in this section.

Executive Chef

The executive chef, sometimes called *chef*, is the person in charge of the kitchen(s) and is often responsible for multiple food outlets. The executive chef is a member of the management team, in charge of all aspects of food production, from menu planning to purchasing, costing, and planning work schedules.

As the number one in the kitchen, he or she is in a challenging position, responsible altogether for quality, consistency, and financial results. Hygiene control is also high on his or her list of priorities, as all products and processes in the kitchen must be risk-free for the customer's health and well-being. The executive chef can be considered as one of the main pillars of food and beverage: without his or her guidance and supervision, quality and consistency could very well be *hit and miss*: on good days, great quality dishes, made with fresh products, and on other days, the opposite!

The main tasks of the executive chef are:

- Menu creation and updates
- Management of all aspects of kitchen staff
- Staff selection, recruitment, and training
- Sourcing, ordering, and purchasing food products
- Inventory control
- Ensure consistency in financial results, the food cost percentage being the kitchen's main benchmark

---

[8] https://en.wikipedia.org/wiki/Le_guide_culinaire
[9] https://en.wikipedia.org/wiki/Brigade_de_cuisine

SECTION ONE	JOB OUTLINE

Job Title Executive chef	Dept. Food and beverage

Division Food and beverage	Job Code Manager	Job Level 3

Reports Directly to:
Executive assistant manager in charge of food and beverage

Supervises:
Chief steward, sous chefs, banquet chef

Other Relationships:
All departments of the hotel
Customers/Suppliers

Job Summary/Purpose: In all food and beverage sales outlets, ensure an overall imaginative, varied and high-quality cuisine, in conformity with hotel's standards and the food and beverage policy.
Through strict, sound management, ensure food and beverage profitability while still preserving service quality.

Key Areas: Responsible for production in all restaurants, room service, banqueting, stores and back of the house staff.

SECTION TWO	KEY AREAS

Job Title	Executive chef

Duties and Responsibilities:

PRINCIPAL ACCOUNTABILITIES
ORGANIZATION

1. Organize the department according to the hotel's standards and procedures, and the hotel's food and beverage policy.
2. Plan, coordinate, and control department activities.
3. Manage and train staff in collaboration with the food and beverage manager/ human resources manager, according to predicted activity levels and services to be carried out.
4. In conjunction with the food and beverage manager/purchasing manager, determine supply quality and quantity criteria.
5. With the food and beverage manager/purchasing manager, participate in selecting suppliers.

Figure 3.17 Executive chef's job description

6. Develop all menus for the different sales outlets, propose them to the food and beverage manager, and renew according to scheduled timetable.
7. Develop standard recipes: portions, ingredients, presentation, and service guidelines.
8. Strictly apply and ensure application of procedures and regulations concerning hygiene and safety.
9. Participate in department inventories at scheduled times.

MANAGEMENT

1. Participate in drawing up the department's budget: food costs, personnel expenses, charges, and so on.
2. In conjunction with the purchasing manager, control supplies: cost, quality/price ratio, size of orders, storage conditions.
3. Make sure that all merchandise is used before the freshness date expires, and adapt stock levels and production to predicted activity levels.
4. Make sure that standard recipes are respected.
5. Control department costs and charges.
6. Make any suggestion to the food and beverage manager likely to improve department profitability.

QUALITY

1. Make sure that all merchandise used is fresh and of high quality.
2. Control storage, preparation, and fabrication methods.
3. Adapt services to staff qualification levels, emphasizing a simple but high-quality cuisine.
4. Supervise the preparation/pickup of dishes.
5. Make sure quality has the same importance in all sales outlets.
6. Show expertise and imagination in adapting services to product availability/quality and seasonal products.
7. On a daily basis, make suggestions and propose attractive and varied menus, which are likely to renew regular clients' enthusiasm.
8. Personally monitor client satisfaction, and take into account all comments.

SALES AND MARKETING

1. Keep informed on changes in the competition and market, and take this into account when developing both à la carte and set menus.
2. Propose to the food and beverage manager promotional actions, such as theme weeks, product weeks, and so on, which are likely to be selected when the strategic plan is developed.
3. Keep informed on changes in techniques and products and propose to the food and beverage manager any measures likely to improve food and beverage business and renown.

Figure 3.17 (Continued)

SECTION THREE	PERSON SPECIFICATION
Job Title	Executive chef

QUALIFICATIONS/ TRAINING	Hygiene training Service-oriented trainings Computer literate (Word and Excel)
WORK EXPERIENCE	Minimum of 3 years relevant experience in a 5* hotel, and minimum 7 years in this industry
DISPOSITION Leadership, relationships, character, potential	Ability to work under pressure Excellent people skills, hardworking, and disciplined

Figure 3.17 (Continued)

Head Chef

Head chefs are often called chefs de cuisine and have similar duties to those of the executive chef. They usually have far greater responsibility for the preparation and production of food in the various outlets and in banqueting operations.

Sous Chef

Sous chefs are senior cooks with years of experience in most areas of the kitchen; for this reason, they can relieve the executive or head chef. A head chef closely supervises kitchen staff, making sure high standards of production and hygiene are maintained at all times.

Second in command in the kitchen, the sous chef ensures the smoothness of the operation in the department and takes over management during the executive chef's absence.

Typically, the sous chef will have a strong presence during meal services, checking quality of dishes while at the kitchen pass, before they are picked up by the service team.

The main functions of a sous chef are:

- Executive chef's assistance
- Quality control
- Supervises kitchen staff, ensuring compliance to hygiene rules

- Assists chef in menu creation
- Coordinates kitchen sections, establishes work schedules
- Recruitment and staff training
- Kitchen staff evaluation

Chef de Partie

A *partie* could be best translated as a kitchen's section, which is part of Auguste Escoffier's heritage: the fish section, the cold section, or the sauce section, and so on. Section chefs or *chefs de partie* are in charge of particular areas of production: sauce chefs or *saucier*, pastry chefs, fish chefs, roast chefs, vegetable chefs, soups chefs, larder chefs, and relief chefs.

In the kitchen's organizational chart, the chef de partie oversees one section within the kitchen's organization, under the sous chef or executive chef's guidance. The main objective of the chef de partie synchronizes his or her section with the others in the kitchen so that dishes may be assembled in an efficient and timely manner.

Most executive chefs started their training in one or more of those specialist areas, before working their ways up the ranks of the kitchen hierarchy.

Commis de Cuisine

Commis de cuisine prepare and cook food in the different kitchen sections. They also ensure that mise en place is ready on time, and that all kitchen utensils are available and clean. Sometimes named junior cooks, they may be assigned to a specific section and report directly to the chef de partie.

Many commis de cuisine start as apprentices, or trainee cooks, under the direction of the head or second chef. In many countries, such as France, it takes a few years for an apprentice to become a qualified cook.

Chef Garde Manger

Better known as *cold kitchen* chef, the garde manger's responsibility is to ensure the timely production of all cold savory menu items: salads, cold appetizers, carpaccios or tartar, or cheese platters, for example. The garde manger is also in charge of large buffets' presentation; this is typically done with a variety of decorative vegetables and other food items, which may be carved or molded into unique and artistic designs. Ice carving is also a garde manger's discipline.

Pastry Chef

In charge of all sweet menu items, typically one of the most beloved of all the station chefs, particularly for the dishes they are responsible of preparing! The pastry section may also oversee the production of baked goods, such as breads and pastries. Sweet breads and croissants are the breakfast bounty of pastry chefs, and sophisticated chocolates and petit fours provide an elegant proof that this is an artistic discipline demanding years of training before reaching excellence.

Figure 3.18 Pastry chef at Georges Blanc's three Michelin star restaurant, presenting his latest sugar creations

Chief Baker

A position found more and more in luxury hotels and fine-dining restaurants producing their own bread and *viennoiseries*, the chief baker is responsible for this section's operations. In many organizations, he or she reports to the pastry chef.

Figure 3.19 Homemade bread, an excellent way to showcase quality and increase value in luxury establishments

The stewarding department

Keywords
Chief steward
Supervisor
Dish, pot washer

Chief Steward

The chief steward oversees the least visible part of food and beverage, which is nevertheless extremely important for a smooth food and beverage operation. In fact, without a stewarding department, food and beverage operations could just not take place.

The scope of the stewarding department extends from providing cutlery, crockery, and service equipment to the restaurant and kitchen, to ensuring compliance in hygiene standards throughout the kitchens, under the executive chef's guidance.

The department is mainly responsible for:

- Cleanliness of the BOH: disinfection of kitchens, storerooms, walk-in fridges and freezers, and all related equipment

- Glassware, chinaware, and cutlery stocks
- Inventory of chemical cleaning products
- Maintenance of dishwashing machines
- Pest control; although in some establishments, this will be jointly managed with the maintenance department

Figure 3.20 The stewarding team at the Empire Hotel in Brunei

Stewarding departmental structure

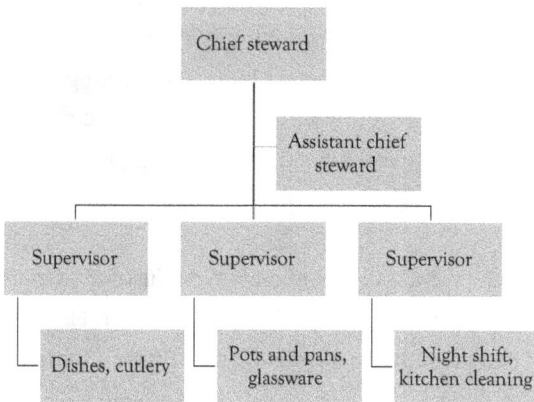

Figure 3.21 Stewarding department organizational chart

Stewarding Supervisor

The stewarding supervisor has the overall charge of the team of stewards and is responsible for seeing that all the equipment and kitchen utensils necessary for service are available in the right quantities. The supervisor will usually oversee a particular shift or section within the stewarding department: morning, afternoon, or night shift. Sections include *pots and pans*, dishwashing, cutlery, or glassware handling. The night shift stewarding supervisor is in charge of deep cleaning of the kitchens during the night, as it is often the only moment of the day they can be accessed by the stewarding department. They also help with the compilation of duty rosters or schedules, holiday lists, and may relieve the chief steward on off days.

Dish, Pot Washer

Also called a kitchen steward, his or her main function is to wash dishes, kitchen equipment, and utensils, to help staff keep high standards of hygiene. Other duties may also be assigned, related to the BOH's cleanliness.

The Menu

The menu is the center point of any food and beverage establishment; that is the reason it should be carefully designed by management. The executive chef has the prime responsibility in deciding what should be on the menu, although the food and beverage director's collaboration will be required for determining adequate selling prices, setting levels of profitability, and for making sure the menu is in line with the restaurant's concept.

You can tell a lot about the restaurant by just looking at the menu; it is a powerful marketing tool and should make an effective statement and reflect the restaurant's concept and service style. From an operational standpoint, the menu is a determinant for absolutely all aspects of the establishment's activities: from the size of kitchen to staffing, types of products purchased, equipment, required skills, number and profiles of staff to be selected and recruited.

The primary selling tool of any establishment, the menu is a legal contract binding the food and beverage operator with the guest; this is why, Truth-in-Menu laws[10] protect restaurant customers.

Menu Types

Table d'hôte

It is common in most fine-dining, luxury operations to feature a *Table d'hôte* menu, which offers restricted, small number of courses, with a fixed selling price. A good example of this is the concept of *formula* offered in a restaurant, mainly at lunchtime: starter + main course or main course + dessert, with pre-determined prices. It is also the format of choice for banquets, as operational constraints do not allow à la carte service for a large number of customers. When used during a banquet, it is commonly referred to as a *set menu*.

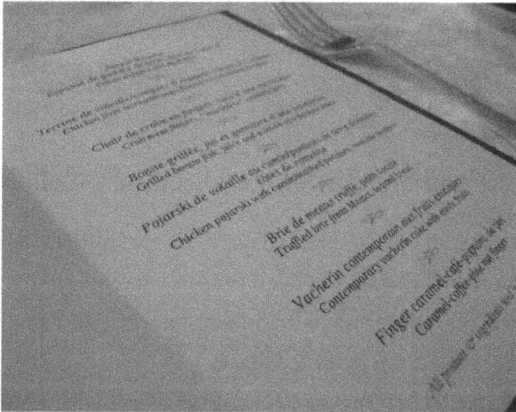

Figure 3.22 Example of set menu used for a small banquet

À la carte

Most restaurants will offer an à la carte menu, with more options to choose from compared to the table d'hôte format. À la carte menu items will usually be priced higher than formulas, as an incentive for guests to choose the latter, which represents a lesser strain on the kitchen. All à la carte dishes being prepared to order, this service requires a well-organized mise en place of all necessary ingredients.

---

[10] Truth-in-Menu law protects the consumer by ensuring that the information provided about menu items is accurate and conforms to local or national regulations.

Fine-dining restaurants often feature a combination of à la carte items, special dishes of the day, and table d'hôte menu proposals so that repeat guests may have a more affordable option, which is renewed daily, according to the chef's inspiration and mood. Special dishes of the day are also a great way for chefs to test new dishes, in view of future menu changes. Menu change, in a luxury operation, will often follow seasonality; from two to four times a year, new dishes should be proposed. Additionally, special seasonal promotions may be added to the à la carte offer: for example, a food promotion on shellfish, game or asparagus, or another seasonal product. Those promotions are usually appreciated by most customers, as they contribute to putting forward an image of freshness.

From a food and beverage control point of view, à la carte is operationally more difficult to control, especially if the menu is large, as many different ingredients are used in the production process. It is the chef's responsibility to make sure that they elaborate a menu that will match refrigerator capacity and limit wastage to the minimum, preserving the operational budgeted food cost.

Chef and Food and Beverage Director's Collaboration

Creating the menu that is best adapted to the outlet's target market requires input from both the chef and the food and beverage director. It is an ongoing collaborative task, which takes patience and analytical skills, as it is primarily based on guest feedback.

Although many chefs meet and exchange words with a few restaurant guests during or after the service, most of the constructive feedback is collected by the restaurant staff, and not necessarily by management. Communication is the key here, to make sure that all feedback is collected during each service and shared with management during service briefings. Additionally, product sales should be analyzed regularly by management, so as to assess the popularity and profitability of each dish.

Based on this information, chefs will compile new menus, on average three to four times per year, and propose selling prices based on recipe costing sheets (see Chapter 5). The food and beverage manager's task will be to validate or adjust those price proposals, according to the restaurant's competition and also take part in the writing of the menu's descriptions and translations whenever it is necessary.

General Principles of Menu Planning and Design

In order to maximize the menu's efficiency as a sales tool, there are a few principles for creating menus. The first one is to truly understand the customer's expectations. Although it sounds easy and quite logical, I have witnessed many examples in which the items on the menu reflected the chef's tastes rather than the customers'.

Knowing customers' demographics is crucial: age range, nationality, sex, the purpose of their visit to your establishment: business, leisure, or cultural. For example, a business lunch proposal will need to be executed in a short time, and light, beautifully presented items should be favored.

The number of guests also is a determinant factor: are you preparing for a large banquet, or à la carte? À la carte for two is a very different matter compared to a banquet preparation for 500 guests.

Taking all the aforementioned into consideration, the menu will be built in accordance with the availability of products. In most of the Western world, virtually, any product can be delivered to a hotel; however, getting your hands on tomatoes can be challenging if you are operating in, for instance, Bora Bora or in Raiatea, in the Society Islands of the French Polynesian archipelago.

In those locations, if you have missed the cargo boat's shipment on Tuesday, then you will have to wait until next week to use fresh tomatoes on the menu. Hence, the use of huge walk-in freezing containers on most tropical islands.

Seasonality, as well as what is now referred to as *locavorism*[11] is also key in today's menu design. Food businesses located in remote areas

[11] The word locavore was coined in 2005 on the analogy of carnivore, *flesh eater* (which most dictionaries prefer to *meat eater* because the Latin caro is translated as *flesh*, but nobody eats fattening flesh these days), and herbivore, *plant eater*. The suffix -vorous means *eating, devouring* and spawned the adjective *voracious*.

The coiner is Jessica Prentice, who had left a job at the Ferry Plaza Farmers Market in San Francisco to write a book about *food and the hunger for connection*. While working on that, she decided to urge people in the Bay Area to eat local food for a month; Olivia Wu, a food writer for *The Chronicle*, challenged her to come up with a name for what Prentice had been calling the nearby foodshed, I presume on the analogy of *watershed*. She promptly melded the Latin locus, place, with vorare, *swallow, devour* and (gulp!) there was locavore, the noun that became the Oxford American Dictionary's word of the year for 2007. https://nytimes.com/2008/10/12/magazine/12wwln-safire-t.html

need to take extra care to consider the availability of fresh food and transportation costs.

Good food knowledge is an essential part of menu planning. A planner needs to be familiar with:

- The variety of food products available
- The differing quality characteristics of food
- The seasonal availability of food
- The availability of reliable food suppliers
- How food products are best packaged, transported, stored, and preserved

Menu planning should translate the restaurant's concept and bring it to life for the customers, in all aspects of the service experience. I have seen numerous examples of *international restaurants* proposing cuisines from all around the world; this can be quite confusing and lack authenticity. Most guests looking for luxury features will prefer a smaller offer with a focus on quality and authenticity, rather than quantity of products available. Having a hundred dishes on the menu also puts an additional load on the purchasing department, responsible for sourcing many references, without a guarantee to have a continuous supply.

The operator and the chefs should also ask themselves: is the menu adapted to the market that is targeted? It is quite different to cater for in-house hotel guests or to local residents, who will often come to the restaurant for different reasons and with a more limited spending power. All this has to be carefully studied when designing the offer.

All these aspects should be considered without forgetting the main objective of a restaurant, or any other business: the need for profitability. Two whole chapters of the book (Chapters 4 and 5) are dedicated to the mechanisms and control systems that are associated with recipe costing and menu selling prices.

Menu design is the next point that comes after creating the dishes and costing them out: which material should be used and how should the dishes be described and translated. The choice of menu material is crucial and should be based on durability, ease of use, and cost effectiveness. Quality and presentation should not be overlooked, for example, cheap-looking materials should be avoided, and staff should be taking great care in checking each menu for cleanliness prior to the service.

Menu presentation must be impeccable, without spelling mistakes, easy to read, and it should reflect the restaurant's identity and image. It takes, on average, two minutes for a customer to read, or rather *eye scan* a menu,[12] which means that whatever needs to be communicated has to be done efficiently and swiftly.

In my experience, it is usually a good idea to invest in a high-quality laser printer to print menus as needed and have the menu cover done by an outside printer. In this way, menu changes can be done without having to reprint the whole covers, which may be very costly.

> *Luxury hospitality's inside story: menu creation at the Hiram Bingham train, Cusco to Machu Picchu*
>
> During my tenure with Belmond hotels in Peru, I had the responsibility of developing menus for an all-new experience in the country: a gastronomic train ride from Cusco to the sacred site of Machu Picchu, and back. The executive chef and I set to work on this project for months before the launch of the train; it was highly challenging and fun to accommodate the food and beverage offer to this new premium service, created specifically for the Hotel Monasterio's guests.

Figure 3.23 Welcome aboard The Hiram Bingham train, a luxury catering experience for Machu Picchu visitors

---

[12] Bates 2004.

This is what the fine-dining experience looks like:

8 a.m.: Departure from the Hotel Monasterio to the Poroy Train Station

8.30 a.m.: Welcome drink offered at the train station, at the sound of a folkloric local band

Hiram Bingham train departs from Poroy Station to Aguas Calientes. Guides are present on board the train and stop by the tables to comment on the breathtaking scenery.

• Brunch on the Hiram Bingham, four-course table d'hôte menu

1 p.m.: Arrival at Machu Picchu site, welcome with a glass of sparkling wine

Guided visit of the citadel, in small groups

4.30 p.m.: English-style afternoon tea at the Machu Picchu Sanctuary Lodge,[13] a well-earned, delicious, sweet moment, after quite some exercise going up and down the ruins

Figure 3.24 The afternoon tea served at the Machu Picchu Sanctuary Lodge

---

[13] Machu Picchu Sanctuary-Lodge is a 31-room luxury hotel situated at the entrance to the Machu Picchu Inca citadel. It is the only hotel at this World Heritage Site, and can be accessed by foot or by rail: https://belmond.com/hotels/south-america/peru/machu-picchu/belmond-sanctuary-lodge/about

6:00 p.m.: Hiram Bingham train departs from Aguas Calientes Machu Picchu to Cusco, Poroy Station
• Aperitif: Pisco Sour, Peru's national cocktail
Gastronomic four-course dinner on the train, to the sounds of local Peruvian bands playing in the bar car.

The main difficulties of setting up this project were logistics and product availability. We had to establish tight schedules and a reliable transportation system for daily supply of the tableware and food products, transiting on the mountainous Andean roads before arriving at the station.

Fortunately, the professional washing machine on the kitchen car helped us greatly as we did not have to offload all the tableware after each trip. This was done on a weekly basis, so all equipment could be inventoried, and any missing items would then be replaced by the chief steward. The chinaware and glassware breakage rate were quite high, but that was expected on such an operation.

Local products were sourced, such as Andean smoked trout, which worked great for starters and required little handling on the train. Alpaca, a very tasty and lean meat, very popular in Peru, was sourced as well, providing typical products originating from the region.

Peru has a frontier with Brazil on its Eastern front, enjoying a tropical climate, so we were able to source a great variety of interesting fruits, such as the extraordinary lucuma.[14] This fruit, which only grows in the Andes, was the main ingredient for a lucuma mousse, a tasty and light dessert, perfect for the return dinner. One of the dishes also featured Huayro potato, one of the thousands of varieties found in Peru.

Kitchen onboard the train was limited in space to one wagon, so it was used as a *finishing kitchen*, while the main production was realized in both Hotel Monasterio and Belmond Machu Picchu Sanctuary Lodge, and later transported to the two train stations.

---

[14] Pouteria lucuma is a species of tree in the family Sapotaceae, cultivated for its fruit, the lúcuma. It is native to the Andean valleys of Chile, Ecuador, and Peru (Wikipedia).

Styles of Service in Food and Beverage

Silver Spoon Service

Silver spoon service finds its origins before restaurants made their first apparition in Paris a few years prior to the French revolution in 1789. This style of service, costly and labor-intensive, was progressively replaced in the early 1900s, first by Russian-style service, also known as guéridon, and then by American or plated service during the second half of the 20th century.

There are two types of silver services: the English service (also called silver spoon service) or the French service (also called semi-silver service). In both styles, food is displayed on silver platters, which are presented to each guest, from the left side. Food portions are then served, clockwise around the table.

English Service

As seen in the following figure, the platter is presented to the left of the guest, and the waiter or waitress performs the service from the platter to the plate. This style of service usually requires several waiters or waitresses, who will follow each other and present the main ingredients (fish, meat) and the garnishes successively.

This type of service is still in used today, for VIP events or even banquets.

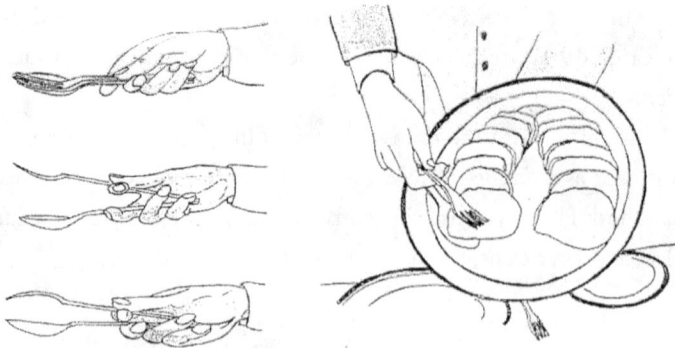

Figure 3.25 English-style service

French Service

French-style service is similar to English-style service, with the exception that the guest helps himself or herself from the platter while it is presented to him or her.

This type of service may still be used today for VIP events, or small-sized banquets; however, it is not as practical and cost-effective as English-style service.

Russian-Style Service or Guéridon

This style of service is particularly used in fine-dining restaurants: carving, fileting, flambéing, presenting and portioning cheese, or desserts on a trolley. All these are examples of guéridon service (guéridon means *small side table* in French).

The advantage of guéridon service is that it brings animation into the restaurant, often generating additional sales. Guests who see this type of animation are most likely to order the same dish themselves and enjoy the show right at their table. This is particularly true with flambeed desserts such as the famous *crêpe Suzette* for example.

Figure 3.26 Guéridon cheese service

American-Style Service or Plated

Plated service started being the industry's norm in the 1960s when the time spent for meals at a restaurant started to decrease dramatically, a trend that is still ongoing today. Another reason for this evolution is that chefs started to use dish presentation as a way to express their culinary art. The dish itself conveys a message, and ultra-mediatization of chefs with TV shows such as *Top chef* and many others strengthened that trend. Diners today, even before they smell the dish as it is being served, will capture it on their smartphone and post a picture of it on Instagram or another social network … the *food porn* movement seems to be here to stay.

From an operational and financial point of view, plated service allows faster service and lower labor costs, as less staff is required to wait on tables and may also be increased. Food cost can benefit from plated service as well, as portion control is made possible through the use of recipe costing sheets.

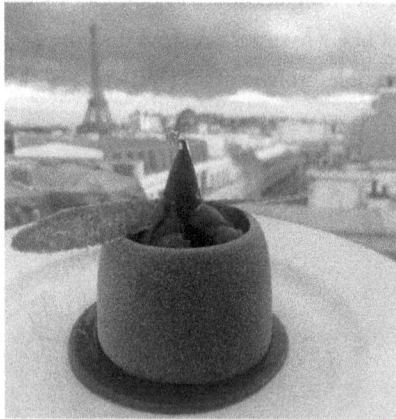

Figure 3.27 Signature dessert of Michelin-starred L'Oiseau Blanc restaurant at the Peninsula Hotel in Paris

Buffet Service

Buffet service is most effective for larger groups of guests, as it offers a great variety of food and beverage options. Moreover, it is a cost-effective type of service, because less waiting staff is required, although clearing and restocking duties should not be overlooked by management when servicing a buffet.

Presentation is of utmost importance when setting up a buffet, and it offers many opportunities to showcase the kitchen team's talents. Buffet displays should be attractive to the eye, but also functional as they often cater to very large groups. Chefs and waiting staff need to be vigilant so that the buffet looks clean and stocked at all times during service.

Figure 3.28 Fruit display used as buffet decoration

For an effective food cost control, the *ABC method* should be used when setting up a buffet: 20 percent of most expensive items, 20 percent of medium-priced items, 60 percent of cheaper items are displayed, and containers should be of small to medium size to avoid wastage.

Chafing dishes are a specific equipment used for buffets, in order to keep food products warm. They should be refilled often so that the aspect of food is always highly presentable. Buffets in general and the use of chafing dishes refilled regularly allow a more effective control of the cost of food for more expensive products, such as seafood for example.

To guarantee a smooth service, a buffet *line* should be set up for each hundred guests. For a more effective guest experience and swifter service, live cooking stations are also often integrated in the buffet.

In order to be cost-effective, a buffet will usually be proposed for a minimum of 30 guests.

The Covid crisis has brought a stop to many buffet operations in many countries, as contactless interactions become the new norm, in order to avoid contamination risks. Buffet service will have to be totally reinvented in order to survive in future: smaller displays, smaller buffets lines spread throughout the outlet, implementation of reinforced hygiene protection during service are some of the solutions that will be used in the industry.

Figure 3.29 Buffet line

Luxury hospitality's inside story: grand wedding celebrations at the Empire Hotel, Brunei

One of the food and beverage department's most profitable activity is banqueting. The reason for this is that unlike an à la carte restaurant, the number of guests is known in advance, as well as the date and time of the event.

Of course, those are subject to many changes, even last-minute ones, before the event actually takes place; however, those are prevented by a contract that is signed by the guest as the banquet proposal is approved.

There is also an economy of scale effect, as kitchen production for large numbers of guests costs less per dish, staff costs are also lower, as the ratio of staff to guests is lesser than in an à la carte restaurant. Banqueting service is usually less complex in technical terms, so less service skills are required than in formal fine-dining à la carte service.

Brunei's Empire Hotel has large and beautifully decorated luxurious banqueting installations, the largest and most luxurious is called the Grand Hall, located outside of the main building, featuring a private entrance just in front of the shoreline. Definitely the perfect setting for high-profile weddings!

Figure 3.30 The Grand Hall entrance at the Empire Hotel in Brunei

The majority of weddings are booked six months in advance, and most of the time, the main theme is either Malay or Chinese style. Each function hosts between 1,500 and 2,000 seated guests. The particularity of these functions is that no alcohol is served, respecting the laws of the country.

The conference and banqueting team is very well experienced with this type of events, which involve most of the hotel's departments. In order to ensure accurate communication of the many details pertaining to an event, a banquet event order is drafted for each function, at least 48 hours before the event takes place. These are internal documents describing all the functions' details, with great accuracy. Those documents must be shared among all the hotel's departments so that guests' expectations and all technical details can be relayed with utmost accuracy to all the relevant heads of department. This is the only way to ensure perfect coordination on the day of the event. Miscommunication is really a banquet's worst enemy, for example, a menu change requested by the guest two days prior to the event, which is not communicated to the kitchen can have disastrous consequences on the event's outcome.

The first contact with the guest is usually made through the hotel's conference and banqueting sales department. The conference and banqueting department in large hotels such as The Empire Hotel falls under the authority of the food and beverage management, and for very large events, sometimes including members of the Royal family or other VIPs, food and manager and assistants' presence is also required.

In this hotel, with 21 banqueting rooms ranging from small meetings rooms to the Grand Hall, holding a maximum capacity of 2,000 seated guests, the banqueting revenue represents half of the overall food and beverage department's income. It is, therefore, very important to have a team of experienced sales coordinators and a well-trained banqueting team in both kitchen and service.

The main role of sales coordinators is to meet with the organizers, in order to get all the technical details and take note of any special requests from the guest. At times, the coordinators will also recommend third-party contractors for decoration or animation services, which cannot be performed in house.

Within the conference and banqueting department, an audiovisual team is in charge of handling any guest's requirements such as video projections, or installing a sound system, a light show or translation booths for example. Audiovisual technicians carry out more technical meetings with the organizer too, to discuss any sound, projection, or lighting requirements.

Menu choices, such as the example shown next, are a part of the banquet kit, which is presented to event organizers during the planning meeting:

Appetizer

Red Ruby Plateau

Chilled Crab Meat Salad, On Fresh Fruits and
Avocado Salad, Topped Mango Mayonnaise

Between

Ginseng and Chicken Soup

Double-Boiled, Conpoy, Red Dates, and Wild Mushrooms

Experience

Blue Ocean Prawn

Stir-Fried with Asparagus, in X.O Sauce

Main

Empire Chicken, Honey Roasted, accompanied
with crispy Prawn Crackers

Ocean Fish, Deep-fried with Sweet Citrus and Lychee Sauce

Abalone Mushroom, Braised with Seasonal
Vegetables, in Golden Oyster Sauce

Fragrant Rice, Wok-Fried with Minced Chicken and Spring Onion

Sweet

Chilled Red Dates with Sea Coconut and Snow Fungus Chinese Tea

Figure 3.31 Banqueting menu offer

The conference and banqueting director holds a key role, as the
liaison between the client and the operational food and beverage team.
They are involved from the first contact until sometimes weeks after
the event, for feedback collection and settling of invoices.

Large weddings such as the one described are a common occur-
rence, so the food and beverage management team is quite well
rehearsed. The first and most important priority is staffing: finding
enough staff in Brunei to ensure exceptional service for 2,000 can be
a challenge.

For such an event, a minimum of 200 waiters or waitresses are required, representing a ratio of one waiter or waitress for 10 guests, or one round table. Brunei is a tiny country, and the Empire Hotel is the only luxury establishment in the country, so whenever a large wedding takes place, most available staff in the country is sought after. The main challenge is that most of the part-time staff are non-Bruneians and are on short visit visas in the country. This adds complexity to the recruitment process, as the personnel are often new to the luxury hotel industry and its quality standards. For this reason, training sessions have to be carried out on a weekly basis, prior to each event.

Senior and middle management presence throughout the whole function is required too, in order to prevent any service issues and to react efficiently in case of a problem.

Facing that ongoing staffing challenge, our team had developed a part-timers' address book, which was updated as often as possible. Besides the difficulties with the lack of training in luxury standards, language barriers are also common, to overcome these issues the food and beverage department has developed an ongoing training effort for casual staff, overseen by two of the three food and beverage assistant managers.

A pre-event meeting systematically takes place on a weekly basis, to review any technical aspects from decoration contractors, audiovisual requirements, security, timings, and so on, and to make sure all the departments are perfectly coordinated, and that communication is flowing. The food and service part, technically speaking for an event such as a wedding, is not very complex, as it is performed in a pre-served-style family style (see the following picture of a table setup). However, it requires a great deal of organization to make sure all guests are served promptly and accurately.

Service is performed in a *wave* style, which consists in having all the waiters or waitresses start from one end of the room and move progressively to the other end, being guided by the banquet supervisors, who are placed in the different sections of the Grand Hall.

Figure 3.32 Malay-style chafing dish, placed at the center of the table during Malay- or Chinese-style weddings

During those functions, most of the outlet supervisors and managers are requested to help the banqueting department in the supervision tasks, so after completing their regular shift, most of them are given the responsibility for the event's coordination, including the service waves. This also constitutes an additional remuneration for the managers involved. A few days before any event, decoration is delivered, most of the time custom designed for the occasion by outside contractors. Installation can take a few days sometimes, and the hotel's maintenance department will be required.

Food production, overseen by the banquet chef, started the day before, in the large banqueting kitchen conveniently located in the BOH of the Grand Hall.

After the event, the service and stewarding team dismantle the function room, which on many occasions has to be reset for another event, such as a conference or a breakfast early the next morning.

The conference and banqueting department then calls for a post-event debriefing meeting with the various heads of department of the hotel, to share any insights on the event's organization, and most importantly, share guest comments, which are the base for future operational improvement.

Figure 3.33 Royal wedding decoration

Figure 3.34 Wedding banquet served for 1,500 guests at the Empire Hotel, Brunei

Food and Beverage Outlets

In this section are described the most common outlets, also named *points of sales* found in hotels. There are of course numerous categories of food and beverage outlets, and many of them overlap, making any official classification highly challenging.

Keywords	
À la carte restaurant	Lounges and bars
Fine dining	Room service, in-room dining
Specialty and themed	Banqueting
All-day dining, coffee shop	Conference and meetings
	Delicatessen, takeaways

À la Carte Restaurant

The definition of an à la carte fits most food and beverage outlets: the main feature is a menu offering various individually priced food and beverage items. This offer is often completed by specials of the day, suggestions, and set menus.

Fine-Dining Restaurant

Sometimes referred to as a *gastronomical* restaurant, generally featuring some elements of formal service, with an important emphasis on cuisine or chef's personality. This type of outlet is most likely to offer à la carte menu options of a high standard, thus with a price range that is higher than average.

The most renowned restaurants in this category may be awarded specific distinctions, such as one, two, or three star(s) in the Michelin guide, which is a worldwide reference, and was created in 1900. The highest rating is of three-star Michelin, and there are only a few establishments with such a grading, seven of them being in the United States.[15]

---

[15] https://guide.michelin.com/us/en/restaurants/3-stars-michelin

Figure 3.35 The three Michelin star restaurant Le Pré Catelan near Paris

Specialty and Themed Restaurant

National, regional character or cuisine is featured in this type of outlet: Chinese, Japanese, Mexican, Italian, and so on. Food, beverages, décor, and staff's uniforms reflect the restaurant's identity or concept, representing a particular cuisine or part of the world through its gastronomy. The food and beverage offer may be à la carte, or buffet, or even both.

All-Day Dining, Coffee Shop

In most hotels, this outlet is the food and beverage outlet offering wider menu variety, featuring longer hours of operations. As the name suggests, this type of outlet is usually open from early in the morning, for breakfast service, until around 10 or 11 p.m. for dinner service. Hotel coffee shops often feature buffets and a large number of seats so as to accommodate most hotel guests, in one, two, or even three seatings for breakfast service.

Lounge, Bar

Lounges offer food and beverage in a cozy setting and relaxed surroundings. They are often adjacent to the hotel's lobby or to a restaurant within the establishment. The most common is the lobby lounge, adjacent to the hotel's lobby, which is staffed by the food and beverage team.

A cocktail, champagne, cognac, or cigar lounge may be placed near a restaurant so that diners may enjoy a pre-dinner drink, or an after-dinner digestif with a cigar. Executive club lounges are usually found in larger luxury hotels, their access is privatized for guests staying in a particular section of the hotel, such as suites. Executive lounges offer services such as check in, check out, breakfast, cocktails, afternoon tea, or light snacks. They are usually operated and supervised by the food and beverage department.

Bars are often a component of lounges and can also be found in swimming pools, on golf courses or beaches, spas, in special events, and so on. Bars that are located in the BOH can also be found in food and beverage operations: dispense bars, used mainly in the case of all-day dining or banqueting. The food and beverage offer will include most alcoholic and non-alcoholic drinks, and a range of wines. A limited snack menu usually complements the offer.

Figure 3.36 Lobby bar of the Hotel Monasterio in Cusco, Peru

Room Service, In-Room Dining

Room service of all meals and beverages throughout the day is the norm for first-class establishments. In some establishments, room service may be limited to early morning teas and breakfasts with the provision of in-room mini bars and tea and coffee facilities.

The floor or room service staff is responsible for service to all the hotel's rooms, 24 hours a day in most luxury hotels. Hotels in this category also propose an in-room butler service, for exclusive service in the guest room. In addition to food and beverage services, a butler may propose other services such as handling personal luggage, bath preparation, valet laundry service, or private bartending.

Figure 3.37 Tahitian canoe-style room service

Delicatessen, Takeaway Shop

A delicatessen is often located within reach of non-hotel guests, nearby the main lobby, as it offers the food and beverage department an opportunity to showcase fresh, homemade products, such as pastries, chocolates, or salads, and sandwiches.

This type of outlet is a great way to market the food and beverage offer outside the hotel, as the convenience of takeaway usually attracts many local customers.

Luxury hospitality's inside story: Pantai and Zen Pavilion restaurants' opening at The Empire Hotel, Brunei

One of food and beverage management's most exciting experience is being given the responsibility to create and design a new outlet. In the Pantai and Zen Pavilion case, the challenge was double: turn a declining seaside restaurant into two modern and luxurious food and beverage venues: Pantai, a Chinese seafood barbeque, and Zen Pavilion, an intimate and sleek Japanese teppanyaki grill.

Full-blown restaurant renovation projects are both time-consuming and expensive, and before heading forward, a whole set of questions must be answered:

Why is a change needed and what is required?

In this case, the answer was rather straightforward: the Pantai restaurant, which means *beach* in Malay, had been operating since the opening of the Empire Hotel in 2000, and the building was no longer looking very appealing to customers. Its seaside location made it subject to faster natural wear, and its kitchen equipment was no longer adapted.

Furthermore, it was lacking a precise concept to attract customers staying in the luxury hotel, who mostly favored the hotel's other outlets. So, after management's recommendations, the ownership of the hotel agreed that it was time to invest in new facilities to bring back patronage to the restaurant.

The second part of the question, *what is required* was answered after many meetings between the executive committee and the owners' representatives. This gave birth to a *concept brief*, a document outlining the main characteristics the future outlet should feature.

Every department's input was necessary, starting of course from food and beverage, but also sales and marketing, housekeeping, maintenance, security, and reception. All meetings pertaining to the outlet renovation were held under careful scrutiny of the director of finance, who determined spending limits and the required rates of returns.

What is the timing?

A crucial element as well is to determine when should the renovation, or construction, start, and how much time is available to complete the project. For the Pantai and Zen Pavilion, a planning and design phase of four months was set, followed by a period of six months for renovation and construction works. The whole project actually took about a year to be completed.

Who will design and execute the project?

Given the variety of options, this can be a difficult question to answer, and many operators make the mistake of thinking the project can be entirely developed *in house*, as most skills are available within a hotel: for example the maintenance and food and beverage departments employ many professionals such as carpenters, plumbers, chefs and so on. The reality is that designing and planning involves a million details, and there is a danger when self-designing your outlet, to make it according to your own tastes rather than adopt a more neutral approach centered on customer targets. It is also beneficial to have an outside company involved so as to have an external view of the overall project.

The decision was made to source three different design companies, specialized in the hotel business. As Brunei does not have many hotels, there was no local design company available; however, many qualitative and reliable options exist in nearby Singapore, Kuala Lumpur, or Bangkok.

After careful evaluation and reference's reviews, it was agreed between the hotel management and owners' representatives that we would work with a company named Studio Q,[16] based in Bangkok.

Based on our initial brief, a far more detailed project outline was compiled by the designer, including schematic designs and architectural elevations of the projected new outlets. The other benefit of working with a design company is that it will coordinate all the

---

[16] http://studioqconcepts.com/

stakeholders interacting in a renovation or construction project: architects, equipment suppliers, building company, contractors, suppliers, government entities, and so on.

Coordinating the various actors is actually the most complex activity to deal with, as there are so many, and that may cause lengthy debates about which color of furniture to buy, or which kitchen equipment need to be purchased, for example. Having a neutral, external consultant designer can greatly ease the decision process, by bringing pre-selected options on the table.

Once the concept has been approved, and all the contractors have been appointed, the next step lies in building a coherent and realistic action plan and timeline so as to make sure deadlines will be met. In reality, delays are frequent; however, they should be kept to a minimum. In most cases, penalties for late completion will be built in the contract between the hotel and the designer so that the latter will do their best to keep a tight schedule and efficient control over the contractors.

After planning and design work, construction of the new outlets was finally on its way. During the planning phase, furniture, tableware, point of sales management system, and kitchen equipment had also been selected and approved for purchase. The lead time on such items, which in most cases had to be imported, is usually around two to three months. Getting everything through customs can also considerably lengthen the process, so additional time had been planned within the timeline.

Kitchen equipment has to be very carefully selected, as it is the bulk of the food and beverage department's capital expenditures (CapEx) list. Kitchen equipment is costly and is generally not to be replaced before many years of operation, such as an oven, an extraction hood, or tabletop counters.

Kitchen equipment costs represent a high percentage of the total cost of a restaurant, but also once a kitchen has been designed in a certain way, it is very difficult to alter its layout. This situation could occur, for example, if the menu has not been given thorough consideration in the planning phase of a project, and six months after opening, operators decide to change the concept of the restaurant, which may involve the purchase of new equipment.

The menu is, therefore, key in the development of the concept and must be approved by all the parties involved, in particular by the executive chef, whose team will have the responsibility to produce the dishes offered when the outlets are functional. I recall a lengthy discussion between the chef and I, he was in favor of installing a pizza oven in the restaurant, and I happened to be against it, as it just did not fit into the concept of Chinese barbeque. That is also when the neutral advice of the kitchen designer comes in handy! We finally agreed not to purchase the oven.

As mentioned earlier, kitchen equipment, similarly to laundry equipment, are heavy-duty, expensive items, and once installed, they are meant to remain in place until their replacement, which should not happen before 20 or 30 years, provided they are maintained adequately. For this reason, we chose to install quality branded equipment, which brought the total cost of the kitchen to around 750,000 U.S dollars, including the teppanyaki griddle and exhaust hoods. The overall cost of the equipment represented about 30 percent of the total project's cost, in line with industry's standards.

Financially speaking, *furniture* comes next on the CapEx list. The particularity of restaurant furniture is that it should be selected and purchased keeping in mind it will be used in a commercial way, so besides the visual aspect, it must also present very high-quality standards, durability, and easiness of cleaning.

In our case, we had an additional constraint, as the restaurants were very close to the sea, so our choice was to buy specifically treated wood and coated fabric to sustain the attacks of the salty breeze. The furniture was custom made in Bangkok, in a record amount of time, and proved to be of high quality.

Visual identity

Our decision had been to offer two restaurants in one, with very distinctive identities: one a cozy, intimate 20-seater teppanyaki grill, and the main outlet, Pantai, featuring a lively show kitchen with buffet islands scattered throughout the restaurant, and offering 120 seats indoor and outdoor.

Our consultant also played a major role here, presenting us with different lines of visuals and logos for the two outlets. Even though nowadays a logo can be created online and it could seem quite easy to draft one, finding the right tone to convey the restaurant's mood is best left to experienced professionals. Based on the logo choice, all items that will be displayed to the guest at any time during their visit were created: menu covers, coasters, takeaway bags, business cards, and so on.

The restaurant eventually opened about two months behind schedule and quickly became a success with both hotel guests and locals, who enjoyed the new buffet formula proposed every night, in a brand-new luxurious décor. The combined efforts were finally paying off, and based on the comments received from our customers, it seemed we had managed to establish a harmonious balance between image, style, operating efficiency, customer comfort, and satisfaction.

Operational considerations

One essential part of the outlet's preopening stages is to imagine and plan how it will be operated once opened: for this, the first step is to develop standards of service (see Chapter 1, Processes, for more details) for all of the operational aspects of a restaurant: when will the restaurant be cleaned, who is in charge of this?, what is the ratio of service staff to guest?, what type of music will be played?, in which way the guest will be greeted?, and so on.

Once all those are developed and approved by management, they will be useful for determining the manning guide, a document reca-pitulating all the positions and their respective numbers required for the operation. For example, for both Pantai and Zen Pavilion, it was decided we would hire a restaurant manager, responsible for both out-lets, assisted by two assistants and five supervisors who would cover the various shifts.

Based on this, corresponding job descriptions had to be drafted; those documents are essential for the recruitment and training processes preceding the opening of the outlet. Future success is highly dependent on this.

The designer and the client need to work closely together in order to ensure that both aesthetics and practicalities are balanced; this requires efficient teamwork, communication to make sure that no detail is left behind:

- Restaurant's exterior: signs, menu displays, entrance, canopies, terrace, patio, landscaping, and so on
- Restaurant's interior: bars, sitting areas, and reception areas, lighting, materials used
- BOH: planning and design, kitchen design, layout and sections, equipment selection and purchasing
- Services considerations: heating, gas, water, electricity, communication, airflow, lighting, acoustics, space programming, layout, guest and service flow

Figure 3.38 Pantai seafood buffet restaurant, and Zen Pavilion featuring Japanese teppanyaki

Banqueting, Meetings, and Conference Department

Not all hotels have a dedicated banqueting, meetings, and conference department. It is mainly found in larger, city hotels, less often in resorts or leisure hotels. The banqueting department is usually under the supervision of the food and beverage department, although in few establishments, a *conference and banqueting* department may be functioning autonomously.

In terms of volume of guests, and food and beverage revenue, the banquet department may be the most important outlet, in food and beverage, and most likely the most profitable too. This is mainly due to the fact that the banqueting operation has a much higher volume of business than other outlets, as many functions may be organized for hundreds, if not thousands of guests, which is the equivalent of weeks or months of business for most restaurants. The other great difference with most restaurants is that banqueting relies on planned events, greatly decreasing the risk of preparing meals that will not be sold, which may happen in an à la carte restaurant.

However, the department relies on a constant sales effort, as banqueting rooms are not always easy to fill, and competition among hotels and other banqueting venues in the area may be quite harsh. In a well-run operation, banqueting revenue can represent half or more of the food and beverage department's revenue, but it is logistically much more challenging than running a restaurant.

The department's greatest challenge is staffing: because many events may take place simultaneously, for large number of guests. Staff requirements may be difficult to fulfill on top of the food and beverage operation. This may raise the question of labor outsourcing, which is often the solution for many hotels.

In this scenario, the banquet manager will call part-time or casual staff, to complete the service team. Banqueting activity may be associated with the hotel's occupancy, for example, when conferences are held, but also relies on local sales such as weddings or other social gatherings. The hotel may also propose organizing and servicing a banquet outside of the hotel. This service is named *outside catering* and demands a very tight organization and strong experience in logistics.

Luxury hospitality's inside story: banqueting, a true lesson in food and beverage

The first job I held in Latin America was in a newly opened Hyatt Regency hotel in Mexico,[17] in the provincial city of Merida, the main city of the state of Yucatan. I was hired as a banqueting assistant manager.

Merida is located a few hours' drive from Cancun, Mexico's tourism Mecca, where I would spend the next four years, after Merida. Since the late 1990s, Merida underwent growth fueled by economic development, but fortunately retained that colonial feel, a total contrast from Cancun, a destination that was chosen by feeding data into a computer.[18]

The banqueting department of a luxury hotel is highly strategic, as it caters to international guests with seminars, conferences, sport events, but also holds an important place in local events: weddings, gatherings, birthday parties, or graduation, which require detailed planning and faultless execution so as to convey a positive image within the local community. Word-of-mouth promotion is very effective, and a single incident could greatly affect the hotel's service reputation.

It is also a challenging, demanding, and interesting type of operation, as most days in banqueting are very different from one another; events can be of all sizes and take place at any time of the day or even the night.

My occupation on any given week was usually made up of multiple small-sized meetings involving local or international companies, conferences, and coffee breaks scattered around the banqueting floors

---

[17] https://hyatt.com/en-US/hotel/mexico/hyatt-regency-merida/merid

[18] Cancun, best-known for its white sand beaches, near-perfect weather, and bright blue waters, is the Acapulco of Mexico's Gulf Coast. Unlike Acapulco, however, Cancun has the modern distinction of being the only city in Mexico whose location was chosen by a computer. In the late 1960s, seeking the ideal spot to build a resort center, the Mexican government entered in factors like average temperatures, beach quality, and accessibility, and—lo and behold—the program spat out set of coordinates near the northeast tip of the Yucatan peninsula. Cancun was born. http://geographia.com/mexico/cancun/index.htm

of the hotel, on the penthouse floor. Many events took place by the swimming pool in winter time, when the weather is a little cooler, as the tropical summer climate just made it too warm to hold any event outside for the rest of the year.

The rhythm of operations would speed up on Friday nights: practically every single week of the year, we catered for a wedding or quinceañera celebration,[19] those types of celebrations, in provincial Mexico, usually involved grand decors, multi-storied cakes, and dancing throughout the night in the hotel's main banqueting venue, the 300-seater Regency hall.

Functions were, on average, planned for 150 to 200 invited guests and were scheduled to begin around 9 p.m., with dinner served at about 10 p.m. At least, that was the plan! However, as working in hospitality teaches you, not one day is ever the same as the other, and you should always be prepared for the unexpected: guests at these weddings or quinceañera celebrations usually started to show up around 10 or 11 p.m. instead of 9 p.m., and dinner would start at around midnight.

In the majority of the cases, the chosen type of service was buffet style. Being in charge of the banqueting department's organization, I was also in charge of counting the number of guests; the best time for that being when they were all seated, that is to say before the dancing floor started to fill up!

On occasion, an additional 50 or 100 guests would show up above the expected numbers, and sometimes much after midnight, when the kitchen team had gone home. In those situations, the trick was to obtain the organizer's green light to prepare extra food so that it could be added to the final bill, before the food on the buffet would run out.

---

[19] The fiesta de quince años (also fiesta de quinceañera, quince años, quinceañera, and quinces) is a celebration of a girl's 15th birthday. It has its cultural roots in Mesoamerica and is widely celebrated today throughout the Americas. The girl celebrating her 15th birthday is a quinceañera (Spanish pronunciation: [kinseaˈɲeɾa]; feminine form of a 15-year-old). In Spanish, and in Latin countries, the term quinceañera is reserved solely for the honoree; in English, primarily in the United States, the term is used to refer to the celebrations and honors surrounding the occasion.

Then, a quick solution had to be found in the BOH: I called the hotel's security department so they would open the banquet kitchen chillers and started looking for ingredients that could be used to prepare an acceptable emergency menu solution. A few minutes later, here we are with my banquet supervisors, preparing grilled chicken for 100 guests.

At this stage, what is required is to feed hungry guests, and what matters most is the outcome of the event and the level of guest satisfaction. In emergency situations such as these, the guests will always be grateful to the hotel for finding a way to solve an unpredicted situation. A hotelier is a little bit as a Swiss knife sometimes, and that includes stepping in the kitchen on some occasions.

Saturdays were quite similar to Fridays, as functions would last until the early morning on Sunday, and we sometimes had to escort the last guests to the entrance of the hotel, at 6 a.m., after having called a taxi. The main reason for this is that our Sunday preparations were just starting: after dismantling the wedding buffet and table setup, it was time to prepare the Regency hall for the next function, usually a baptism celebration.

This type of function was set to start around 11 a.m., so there was not so much time to get ready. The baptisms would officially end after lunchtime, but most of the time, the atmosphere was so pleasant the event lasted until 8 or 9 p.m.! Needless to say, Sunday evening, all the banqueting team headed straight home for a well-earned rest. As far as I was concerned, I would often sleep until noon on Monday, which thankfully was usually my off day.

Luxury hospitality's inside story: outside catering operations in Merida, Mexico

Another important component of a food and beverage department, which is usually well developed in luxury hotels, is outside catering. Similarly to inhouse functions, outside catering operations can take many shapes or forms: cocktails, banquets, buffets, meetings, ranging from a couple of guests on a private beach to dinner service for 2,000–3,000 guests.

The main advantages of developing such operations are mostly visibility in the local market, a showcase of what the food and beverage department can produce outside its walls. Think of the impact of a beautiful and tasty buffet at a wedding party, the guests very likely will want to know who was involved in the preparations, and that may in turn generate additional business for the food and beverage department. So, the added benefit is that access is given to potential customers who may not be your regular patrons in food and beverage; outside catering can, therefore, constitute great publicity if executed faultlessly. The banqueting department being subject to different levels of activity, having an outside catering division will also help diversifying its activities, and generate revenue even if the hotel's function rooms are suffering from low occupancy.

The challenges involved with outside catering are many though, starting with the kitchen's organization: often, the premises for such functions are located in remote areas, without any or limited production facilities. The service team is also facing a logistic constraint, as a large quantity of tableware and equipment need to be brought onsite.

I recall a very busy period in banqueting at the Hyatt Regency Merida, during which the hotel had been practically sold out to a large customs officers conference. The group's three-day program included numerous conferences and meetings, leaving us with the task and responsibility of organizing all of their food and beverage events, in and outside the hotel.

On the last day of their stay, after having served 400 breakfasts in buffet style, the Regency ballroom had to be reset with a totally different theme: *The Clamato*[20] *afternoon*. The decoration was quite lengthy to realize, as it was made of a central buffet exclusively made of fresh vegetables, so the whole banqueting team joined forces in order to complete it just in time for the guests' arrival! The event was a pre-farewell event, a lunch followed by cocktails, before the final

---

[20] Clamato is another name for tomato juice, also called Virgin (no alcohol) or Bloody (with vodka) Mary.

gala dinner, which was to be served in Uxmal,[21] a famous Mayan site, 60 kilometers away from Merida.

The gala dinner consisted of a buffet for 700 guests, set under a very large tent, a must-have precaution, as it often rains in tropical Yucatan, and you cannot just take a chance with weather! Hoping the clouds will go away and rain will not come is just not enough, and not having a B plan can have disastrous consequences with this type of event!

The dinner schedule was tight, every guest had to be served between 7 and 8 p.m., so that they could then watch the sound and light show at the archaeological site.

Most of the kitchen production, for such an event, is realized as much as possible in the hotel's kitchens, as a site such as Uxmal has absolutely no kitchen installations or equipment, even water supply is often a challenge.

Food regeneration, in other words reheating, has to take place on site, so a few trucks were necessary to carry all the equipment, food supplies, tableware, chairs, and table. Logistics also involved the transportation of 100 members of staff who had to be transferred onsite to cater for the event, so a couple of buses were also rented.

Nowadays, as a food and beverage management lecturer in many hotel management schools, I often talk to my students about the importance of par stocks. They represent the quantity of each item you should have on hand at all times, such as food ingredients, drinks, silverware, linen, and so on, in order to run a successful operation and limit the risk of running out of anything. The notion of par stock is even truer in outside catering situations, as absolutely nothing can be overlooked: even if salt and pepper cruets are left behind, this can turn into an operational nightmare, there are no shops around to just go and buy them!

---

[21] Uxmal (Yucatec Maya: Óoxmáal [ó'ʃmáˀl]) is an ancient Maya city of the classical period located in present-day Mexico. It is considered one of the most important archaeological sites of Maya culture, along with Palenque, Chichén, and Calakmul in Mexico, Caracol, and Xunantunich in Belize, and Tikal in Guatemala.
https://en.wikipedia.org/wiki/Uxmal

This particular afternoon, we struggled with our glasses' par stock, as they had to be washed and polished after the Clamato event, in order to be loaded onto the fourth and last truck heading to Uxmal. It always takes longer than expected to wash and reset tableware, so sometimes, it can be a great idea to rent additional equipment, just in case.

As for the Mexican weddings, our guests enjoyed the party so much and had a real hard time to leave the Clamato function, which delayed the departure of our truck, as we were also waiting on the chairs! Again, an additional par stocks of chairs would have made our life much easier!

Roads in Mexico being what they are, and our trucks loaded with fragile tableware, in pouring rain, we got there just in time, when most of the setup had been realized by the team members already in Uxmal.

Needless to say, they were eagerly waiting for our truck containing the 700 chairs: with everyone on board, it took only a few minutes to offload them and have guests seated just in time, and protected from the rain, thanks to the rented tent!

Eventually, the organizer's feedback was excellent; mission had been accomplished, bringing us the satisfaction of a job well done, even if a fair amount of stress was experienced, but that is part of the excitement of luxury hospitality! However, I realized we had played it a little too lean with par stocks, a few minutes more and the event could have gone in a different direction, with food on the buffets and no seats to sit on; fortunately, effective teamwork made everything a success. As always, in these situations, lessons are learned: hire extra equipment, without relying only on the department's par stocks.

Staff, the Industry's Greatest Asset

Throughout the book, we have discussed the importance of staff as the number one ingredient for successful operations in luxury hospitality.

Job descriptions are tools that help determine the best staff profile required to fill a given position, for example, a restaurant manager should have great people skills, an excellent personal presentation, and have two years of experience in a similar position.

Other tools used in the hotel industry are staffing guides, which is basically the human resources budget allocated to a department, informing the reader on the quantity of staff that may be hired for a specific outlet, and their respective lines of report.

Hours of operation	Covers	Service staff
18.00–19.00	80	5
19.00–20.00	120	8
20.00–21.00	100	6
21.00–22.00	100	6

Figure 3.39 Restaurant scheduling according to guest affluence

Productivity standards can be measured by calculating how many tables are served in a given amount of time, as well as many other ratios and indicators on labor hours and expenses (see Chapter 4, The profit and loss statement).

Of course, these are key elements for evaluating the performance of the food and beverage department, although this is mainly a financial tool.

What is much harder to measure than productivity is the impact of staff actions on guest satisfaction: and this is the most important indicators of all, as without consistent guest satisfaction, there is no hotel or restaurant business.

Selection and Recruitment

The luxury hospitality sector, and more particularly food and beverage, relies on qualified labor with a certain set of personality traits, specific knowledge such as foreign languages for example. For these reasons, one of the industry's most critical challenge lies in selection and recruitment. In addition, there are specificities within the luxury sector, which may increase the challenges of finding enough suitable personal to run operations in optimal conditions: lack of attractivity of the hotel industry, long and unsocial work hours, and a high job turnover rate, mainly due to the possibility of job switching or job zapping.

Precise job descriptions greatly help in refining the selection and recruitment process, which is carried out by the food and beverage heads of departments or managers, depending on the position's level. For example, a food and beverage manager would interview potential candidates for a restaurant manager's position, but not necessarily for a commis, a waiter, or waitress position. Depending on the size of the organization, the restaurant supervisor, restaurant assistant manager, or restaurant manager would interview all candidates seeking commis, waiter, or waitress positions.

The role of the human resources department is to pre-select the many applications that are received on a daily basis in most luxury hotels, based on personal presentation or knowledge of foreign languages for example.

I have interviewed many thousands of candidates for very diverse positions and levels of responsibility, and personal attitude has always been my first concern, above level of experience or amount of skills. The success of a luxury operation relies mostly on human interactions and how guests perceive the staff behavior toward them. As a manager, I try to imagine a potential employee's attitude in times of pressure or discomfort, for example, when a guest complaint arises, or any other conflictual situation involving members of staff or guests, or both. An open-minded attitude will probably work best than a *know it all* approach in these instances.

As I was hiring a restaurant manager for the Carlisle Bay Resort,[22] a Leading Hotel of the World[23] located on the island of Antigua, I short-listed a candidate who had an impressive experience as Maître d'hôtel and restaurant supervisor in many luxury properties in the Caribbean. However, he turned up 20 minutes late for the scheduled interview, without taking the trouble to call the hotel or send a message. Needless to say, I was not very impressed, and when he finally showed up for the interview, I noticed his grooming was not up to the expected standards: his shirt had not been ironed and shoes were not polished. One could have said, "well, we are in the Caribbean, so everything should be more relaxed!" To this, I would answer that hotel guests paying around 1,000 U.S. dollars per night to stay at the property deserve the absolute best! I did not hire the candidate, and eventually chose a much less experienced one, who had a

---

[22] https://carlisle-bay.com/
[23] https://lhw.com/

service attitude that coincided more with the expectations; he stayed on in the resort for many years and collected numerous positive guest comments and proved to be a great motivator for the restaurant team.

Food and beverage skills are relatively easy to acquire with daily training and practice; however, negative attitudes or bad habits are much harder to change.

Main Staffing Challenges

Once recruited, the next challenge is to integrate the new collaborator to the team, and for this, careful follow-up is required in order not to leave anyone behind and potentially demotivated. There are countless sources of pressure in the food and beverage industry on any given day, and a small conflict can take large proportions if nothing is done to resolve it.

That is why, communication through the daily departmental briefings is key. Another particularity of food and beverage is that the days are often long and physically demanding, with entry-level salaries tending to be rather low.

Therefore, it is the department head's responsibility to constantly raise the level of attractivity at work. Fortunately, there are many growth opportunities in the hotel industry, and I would always give priority to internal promotions whenever there was a recruitment need in the department.

This has a double benefit: it shows the team members that promotions are accessible to anyone who is interested in growing professionally, and it also decreases the recruitment costs of having to look for staff outside the company.

Making sure that the right candidates are hired is where luxury service starts, as hiring the wrong person can have disastrous consequences on guest service or staff morale within the group. It also puts forward an image of professionalism for the company, which is beneficial for the staff, as they are more likely to remain onboard for a longer period of time.

On the other hand, certain outlets do not experience high staff rotation, as described in the following example. Although this can be beneficial in certain aspects such as repeat guest recognition, or excellent knowledge of the facilities, it can also bring some limitations in the field of flexibility and ability to improve professional practices.

Luxury hospitality's inside story: the delicate art of staff manage-
ment in food and beverage

One of the most complex features of food and beverage management
in the luxury hotel industry is handling staff. Due to the nature of
labor-intensive activities within the department, coupled with the high
level of guest expectations in this kind of establishment, the teams to
be managed can be made of a few hundred collaborators.

One of my first experiences of handling a consequent group of
staff was at the Hyatt Cancun Caribe,[24] a five-star hotel located in the
hotel zone of Cancun, Mexico. I had been given the responsibility of
managing the Blue Bayou restaurant, a fine-dining restaurant featuring Cajun cuisine.[25] Although life as a restaurant manager was a little
less busy than in banqueting, I worked split shifts and often finished
around midnight or one in the morning. The hotel had been around
for 23 years and was one of the first ones ever built in Cancun in
the 1970s.

I was in my late 20s, and it was actually my first time leading a
whole outlet's team, being confronted to the challenge of getting the
job done through other people, without them feeling they were told
to do it.

The FOH team was made of six permanent waiters; most of them
could easily have been my father or grandfather, as they had been
around since the hotel opened, except for two of them who were in
their 30s. On the positive side, they brought a wealth of experience,
and knew all the guests, many of whom were repeaters, year after year.

They also knew all the *tricks of the trade*, and to make things slightly
more challenging for me, the hotel's union representative was on my

---

[24] https://hyatt.com/en-US/hotel/mexico/hyatt-zilara-cancun/cunia

[25] Cajun cuisine (French: cuisine cadienne, [kɥizin kadʒæ̃n]), (Spanish: cocina
acadia) is a style of cooking named for the French-speaking Acadian people
deported by the British from Acadia in Canada, incorporating West African,
French, and Spanish cooking techniques, in the region of Louisiana. Cajun cuisine is sometimes referred to as a rustic cuisine, meaning that it is based on locally
available ingredients, and the preparation is relatively simple.
https://en.wikipedia.org/wiki/Cajun_cuisine

service team. It took a few days before I was, rightly so, labeled as the new manager who wants to change their ways of working. I could clearly understand their thinking: let us see how long this new manager lasts, after all we have seen so many of them before.

Habits die hard, and my first attempts to improve operating standards such as setting up tables, or guest welcome, were met coldly by my new work colleagues. After only a few weeks, they decided I was very tough with them and requested a meeting with the human resources director, the food and beverage director, and myself, to highlight my *harsh and unfair* manners. I thought, "oh no, only a few weeks on the job and I am in trouble!" But, I knew it was for the right cause.

This was my real first professional shock, and I recall coming out of the meeting quite demotivated and hurt, the only thing I wanted to do at that time was to quit! A few days later, after letting things cool down, I decided to not let my emotions overwhelm me too much, it was work after all and no one was sick. I hung on despite the adversity, thinking "if you can't beat them, join them." So, it took some time, but I eventually found ways to join them without compromising on the standards of service. The main thing I realized after that experience was that I should get closer to my team if I wanted to get anywhere, which does not mean we had to instantly become best friends! Participating in football or volleyball matches on the beach after work, going for a taco and a beer together, getting more involved in hotel cross-departmental activities (cleaning beaches, helping associations against poverty, for example). All these activities outside of the strict work environment helped me create a stronger bond with the staff and increase my leadership rating.

Looking back on this period, I have learned many useful lessons that sound obvious to me nowadays; hopefully, they can be helpful to others in the industry, when faced with similar situations, so here is a short list:

- Although it may sound like one of those advices from a personal development book: hang on and do not give up!

- Diplomas do not teach you the *real life*, only life does. I tell this to my current students in hotel management, many times a day.
- Do not jump straight away into a new role and start changing procedures and ways of working, but rather observe what is happening for a while; you will achieve more that way, instead of trying to impose authority through your title.
- Develop empathy for your colleagues, and try to understand if there may be something preventing them from carrying out their work the way they should: lack of equipment, motivation, lack of recognition.
- Learn about the culture you are in before you do anything else; take time for observation.
- Be kind and fair, but keep your boundaries.
- Practice the art of diplomacy; after all, it has avoided countless wars!

Customer Service and Crisis Management

I have shared a few stories throughout the book that show how so many diverse situations can be encountered in the course of a day in the life of a hotelier. After all, as the famous Ritz Carlton Hotels[26] motto says: "we are Ladies and Gentlemen serving Ladies and Gentlemen."[27] However, ladies and gentlemen all have, without exception, good and not so good days. No manager in the service industry should ever forget that and should be practicing keeping your cool during all situations. Far from easy!

I have been witness to many types of traumatic events during my hotel career: hurricanes in Cancun or the Caribbean, huge stones falling from the mountain on a Peru Rail train, landslides, fights in hotels, intoxicated guests, theft, and so on. A hotel is itself a small world, so anything that happens in the *real* world will also happen within the walls of a hotel. So, it helps to be prepared.

---

[26] https://ritzcarlton.com/
[27] https://ritzcarlton.com/en/about/gold-standards

I recall that special night in Cancun, at the Hyatt, when I was called by the reception to face very angry guests, who complained that their next-door neighbors, for some strange reason, had thrown out all their room furniture into the pool seven floors below and were presently busy trashing out the room! It turned out that the room was occupied by four spring breakers who were having the time of their lives in Mexico. A few minutes later, knocking on their door did not achieve much, as they probably did not even hear the knocking.

Somehow, eventually, peace was found, after lengthy negotiations with the troublemakers' rooms. Things finally settled down, and the next morning a round of room inspections was carried out to assess damages and prepare related bills. The next day, many non-spring breaker guests were rightfully wondering about the havoc created the night before; they were expecting apologies from management, and possibly discounts on their hotel stays too! As soon as I walked in the restaurant the next morning, I was straight away spotted by the guests, as one of the managers. I then thought that the day was just starting, and that it would be a long one, dealing with guest complaints!

Just another day in a hotelier's life, and one more example of the diplomatic skills required to succeed in this trade: be absolutely prepared for the unexpected, for any situation, even as absurd as it may seem! They inevitably will happen, it is a part of life, in palaces as in one-star hotels.

Following are some of my favorite crisis management stories, some involving staff, guests, or caused by technical factors.

Luxury hospitality's inside story: the longest minute…

Anyone can surely recall a situation so uncomfortable that seconds seem like hours, or a whole lifetime: one of those moments that remain stuck in the air, as if time had completely stopped, without any intention of starting ever again. There are many potential situations such as these in the hotel industry; but in my view, the story I am about to share here deserves the palm of honor in the "wish I could turn into a very small fly on the wall" category. The year 2013 was a very important one in Brunei, as the Sultanate was assuming the Chairmanship of the

Association of Southeast Asian Nations (ASEAN),[28] and The Empire Hotel, where I was working at the time, was the host hotel and chaired the ASEAN Summit and related summits.[29] Usually quiet and peaceful Brunei was then a bustling place, organizing and hosting world-class summits involving many European and Asian countries, as well as the United States.

My role at the time was "Executive assistant manager in charge of food and beverage." As number two to the general manager, my duty involved being present for any important visit. There were many, as members of the Brunei Royal Family or foreign heads of states were welcomed on a daily basis.

Under the guidance the general manager, a luxury hotel veteran, and diplomatic Irishman, I was taught the tricks of presidential and royal protocols, an object of fascination and excitement to me: being on stage on the red carpet! The most important thing on those occasions is of course to document yourself well before welcoming any VIP to the hotel, so as not to get mixed up with the honorific titles: *Your Majesty* for a president, or the opposite, would definitely not work very well!

One sunny and warm day of 2013, as most days are in Brunei, we were about to receive the Malaysian Prime Minister Dato' Sri Haji Mohammad Najib bin Tun Haji Abdul Razak, head of State of Malaysia. As per the protocol, the general manager and I, along with other members of management, were standing by the glass doors leading into the enormous and glittering lobby of The Empire Hotel.

---

[28] Association of Southeast Asian Nations https://dictionary.cambridge.org/dictionary/english/asean

[29] The ASEAN Summit is a biannual meeting held by the members of the Association of Southeast Asian Nations (ASEAN) in relation to economic, political, security, and socio-cultural development of Southeast Asian countries. In addition, it serves as a prominent regional (Asia) and international (worldwide) conference, with world leaders attending its related summits and meetings to discuss various problems and global issues, strengthening cooperation, and making decisions. The summit has been praised by world leaders for its success and ability to produce results on a global level. https://en.wikipedia.org/wiki/ASEAN_Summit

Figure 3.40 The red carpet is used for all VIP guests, for their arrivals and departures

The head of state protocol is a detailed one, here are its main steps:

- Greeting by the general manager, or the executive assistant manager, or both.
- Escort the visitor to the main lift, located 50 meters away, after crossing the whole reception and lobby area. That part was quite a challenge in itself, as all of the entourage, on average between 35 and 50 persons, wanted to be as close as possible to the main protagonist.
- The lift is *privatized*, which means that a maintenance technician is on standby, blocking all requests made to it. The lift is then programmed to remain with its doors open, until the visitor enters.
- Once inside the lift, a hotel's security agent pushes a button and the lift directly goes up, without possibility of stopping, to the top floor, where the presidential suite is located.
- The visitor is escorted to the suite and wished a pleasant stay by the general manager.

- Members of hotel management then stand by outside the
  suite for a few minutes, awaiting any further instructions,
  and attending to any requirements. No other member of
  staff is usually allowed near the room, for security reasons.
  On those occasions, I would make sure to have my room
  service manager close by as food and beverage is often
  the first request made, and service needs to be of course
  flawless, fast, and highly efficient.

I was feeling confident, as every single detail had been checked, and rechecked, and checked again, many days before the visit, so we were well rehearsed. It was just a typical tropical day in Brunei, although it felt quite cool in the building, because of the energy guzzling air conditioning compressors located under the hotel. Our hotel's monthly electricity bill was around a quarter of a million dollars.

Once we got into the overcrowded lift, the doors closed, and absolutely nothing happened! As discreetly as possible, I slowly bent my head down, to catch a glimpse of our security agent and noticed a hint of stress in his eyes. I immediately thought it was not a good sign.

As we were standing by, the temperature was rising, and I started to feel a drop of sweat forming on my forehead, which slowly went rolling down toward my cheek. In the position I was in, I could barely move an eyelid, so I just stood there and hoped the lift would eventually start!

In my line of vision stood the general manager, silent and motionless as a stone, all was under control! No one spoke, moved, smiled, or expressed any other emotions, and time stood still for a seemingly very long time. Suddenly I felt a slight jerk, the lift was finally moving, although it was in the wrong direction, as it was going down!

At that point I thought, we have reached the bottom, and nothing worse can happen! The poor security agent was now showing signs of stress and was sweating heavily, as he was kneeling down and fiddling about the electric cabinet. It took many more seconds for the lift to slowly start its ascent and eventually make its way up to the seventh floor.

The doors finally opened, and there was a moment of grace, followed by relief when the Prime Minister smiled and said something in Malay, which made his entourage smile. I thought, it looks as though we have avoided the diplomatic incident!

He left the hotel a few nights later, after congratulating the hotel staff and commenting on the excellent service he had enjoyed during his stay; our mission had been accomplished!

Figure 3.41 Prime Minister's arrival at The Empire Hotel

Luxury hospitality's inside story: Queen Beatrix and the capricious Rolls Royce Phantom at the Empire Hotel, Brunei

Let us remain in the Kingdom of Brunei for another royal short story, and the illustration of turning a potentially critical situation into normality, with utmost discretion and without any notice from the guest: another trait of luxury service.

The Empire Hotel is like a small city, opulent, luxurious, and designed around *clean* entertainment: five bars, and even a night club can be found in the hotel, but there is not a drop of alcohol sold anywhere in Brunei. As a consequence, Western tourists are quite rare, and most visitors are there for business reasons, or for a stopover on the way to or back from another South East Asian destination such as Singapore or Kuala Lumpur.

As previously mentioned, 2013 was an intense year because of the various ASEAN summits being held in Brunei, with all types of events taking place, in and out of the property. On January 22, Queen Beatrix, the then Queen of The Netherlands, her son Prince Willem Alexander and his wife Máxima Zorreguieta, visited Brunei for a three-day state visit. This was to be the Queen's last official visit, and of course, this made headlines in the local press.[30]

The Royal family was hosted in the hotel's most prestigious suites, located on the seventh floor, which can be accessed through a private entrance, without having to go through the main lobby.

The program for the day involved a State dinner, followed by a cultural show at the hotel's own theater, a beautiful building adjacent to the hotel, which could host 300 guests. This event was hosted by Brunei's members of the Royal family.

Figure 3.42 The theater at The Empire and Country Club in Brunei

---

[30] http://bt.com.bn/2013/01/22/queen-beatrix-netherlands-visits-brunei

Head of state protocol is to be strictly followed, and as previously mentioned, official and high-profile visits were always handled by the general manager and a member of senior management such as the executive assistant manager or the director of rooms for example. This demanded training and an ability to react to unpredicted situations. Patience was needed too, as one could not always predict the exact times of arrival and departure of the guests. The scorching Borneo heat, coupled with the high humidity, did not make the matter easier, as the management team was dressed in suit and tie all day.

Heads of states and other high-ranking guests on official visits were usually transported in classic style: a vintage Rolls Royce, imposing, robust and sturdy, and custom built for the Sultan of Brunei.

At least one Phantom was built for the Sultan of Brunei; in 1995, it was named Rolls-Royce Phantom V. Three other Phantoms were built between 1995 and 1997, also for the Sultan; they were named Rolls Royce Cloudesque, and sometimes referred to as Rolls-Royce Phantom VII.[31]

Shortly after they had checked into the hotel, I was standing by the private entrance and waiting for the Dutch Royal family. I was advised by the room service manager, who was on standby on the seventh floor, that they were about to come down on the elevator. The two drivers, who were waiting by the Phantom, started getting into motion.

One of them got in the driver's seat and proceeded to start the engine, and strangely, as he was turning the key in the ignition, nothing happened. At that very moment, I realized that this vehicle must have weighted around two tons, and that it would require an army of people to push start it if we had to. Furthermore, it was parked uphill!

---

[31]   Three other Phantoms were built between 1995 and 1997, also by order of the Sultan of Brunei. This car was named Rolls-Royce Cloudesque and sometimes referred to as Rolls-Royce Phantom VII. The exterior is reminiscent of a strand so onhed Phantom V Limousine; the extra length being added at the B-pillar. The boot is redesigned, looking more like that of a Silver Seraph. The headlights were designed in a Silver Cloud III style (but with chromed eyelids), hence the name Cloudesque. https://en.wikipedia.org/wiki/Rolls-Royce_Phantom_VI

Figure 3.43 The Rolls Royce Phantom, used for high-profile visits

A slight feeling of panic starts creeping in, similar to that feeling during my very long lift ride with Malaysian Prime Minister.[32] I stood there quite helpless, and watching the two drivers who started moving about the Rolls, and not looking very worried at all, business as usual it seemed.

One of them opened the trunk, and the second one stuck his head inside, lifted the carpet in the right corner, which was covering a whole bunch of electric cables, he started to fiddle around with them. The second driver went back to the driver's seat, a second after I heard the great sound of the electric starter, the Rolls coughed a black cloud of smoke, and the V12 engine soon was purring like a satisfied old cat.

The dinner service went smoothly, and the theater show started on time and was much appreciated by our guests. Management could go home and rest with the satisfaction of a job well done.

---

[32] See "the longest minute," page 121.

Figure 3.44 Queen Beatrix of The Netherlands at the Empire Hotel in Brunei

Luxury hospitality's inside story: crisis management at Bora Bora Pearl Beach Resort, French Polynesia

Managing food and beverage operations in a luxury hotel is a bit like being an equilibrist, a man on a wire, as no day goes without its share of problems or conflicts, big or small, but all requiring swift solutions.

Many times, the solution is found through effective communication, for example, asking the chef to speed up a particular dish after noticing some signs of impatience at a table. Showing empathy can help too, for example, just taking the time to listen to members of staff, or a guest with a grievance, can avoid a complaint later.

And, there are times, fortunately not too often, when the situation turns into what can be called a crisis. Management is there to control these situations, which happens in all operations, palaces, as well as one-star hotels.

To illustrate this with an example, let us now travel to this beautiful postcard dream destination, Bora Bora, French Polynesia. I worked at the Bora Bora's Pearl Beach hotel, an 80-room resort, member of the Leading Hotels of the World, for two years. The situation I am about to describe took place at the end of 2001; I was at the time the hotel's food and beverage manager and heading a team of about 50 staff.

I must say Bora Bora holds a very special place in my heart for a few reasons; firstly, because my son was born nearby, in Papeete, Tahiti. There was no clinic in Bora Bora, so any expecting mother had to have a pretty good sense of timing, in order to catch an inter-island flight on Air Tahiti to get to the hospital on time! My son flew for the first time, back to Bora Bora, when he was three days old.

Another thing I will never forget about Bora Bora are the colors, which are so much better than even on the best postcards, it is usually the other way around when it comes to touristic brochures! Also, I recall that unique feeling of being at the very end of the world, in such a special place. And, being an enthusiastic scuba diver, the sight of lemon sharks gliding by peacefully is absolutely unforgettable.

French Polynesians have a genuine sense of welcome and hospitality I have never encountered anywhere else, and that goes far beyond the traditional tiaré flower[33] welcome at the airport!

In terms of organizational skills, however, they would honestly sometimes also drive me crazy! As on New Year's Day of 2002, during dinner service at the Tevairoa restaurant. This was the main restaurant of the Bora Bora Pearl Beach Resort, where breakfast, lunch, and dinner were served.

Our New Year's Eve special dinner service had gone pretty well, with a full hotel and restaurant. Most of our guests stayed on the *motu*[34] for dinner, as there were not that many places to go out for a dine around.

The restaurant staff had actually done an amazing job, serving a six-course menu for 150 guests that night, without any major glitch.

---

[33] Gardenia taitensis, also called Tahitian gardenia[2] or tiaré flower, is a species of plant in the family Rubiaceae. It is an evergreen tropical shrub that grows to 4 meter (10 feet) tall and has glossy dark green leaves that are 5–16 centimeters (2–6 inch) long and are oppositely arranged along the stem. https://en.wikipedia.org/wiki/Gardenia_taitensis

[34] Motu, a reef islet formed by broken coral and sand surrounding an atoll. https://en.wikipedia.org/wiki/Motu

The service ended at around 2 a.m. that night, and then it was the staff's turn to celebrate the arrival of 2002. Hotel management was part of the celebration too, around a huge bonfire on the beach, with freshly caught red tuna and mahi-mahi fish being grilled.

Breakfast and lunch service were assured by the morning team, and most of them had not worked the night before. Despite a few members of staff missing for breakfast, and a heavy guest affluence just before closing time, which is perfectly expected on any New Year's Day, there were no major service issues.

Figure 3.45 Tiaré is Tahiti's national flower, used by staff daily and for visitors' welcome

Then came the evening of January 1, 2002, which will always remain in my memory! We were fully booked for the evening, with 120 reservations, most of them programmed between 7 and 8 p.m.

What we call in the hotel jargon the *mise en place*, or *setup*, getting the restaurant or kitchen ready before service is usually done two to three hours before service takes place, meaning that the restaurant staff *should* have shown up around 4 p.m. that day. Well, I guess you know what is coming next: that particular afternoon, no one showed up, not one member of the service team!

I went to the kitchen to see the chef, fearing the worst, and the BOH situation was not better than the front: only one dishwasher was on duty, the chef, and the pastry chef, no one else! That was quite a lean team for five-star service for 120 à la carte covers!

We were quickly submerged by the wave of guests, as all of them showed up shortly after 7 p.m. The evening was, without doubt, a flop, a hotelier or restaurant owner's worst nightmare, when the operation slips out of control in a downward spiral.

Running and sweating, while desperately trying to catch up on the orders of 120 guests, who are understandably trying to get your attention to ask a very basic question: "where is my main course, it has been 45 minutes since I finished my starter!"

In summary, the situation on the *battlefield* that evening looked as such:

- All the 120 hungry guests, understandably tired from New Year's Eve celebrations, and wishing to get an early meal, so that they could retire to the comfort of their over water or garden bungalow.
- An extremely stressed-out chef.
- A lonely dishwasher, who really did the very best he could.
- A pastry chef.
- A somewhat stressed-out food and beverage manager
- The general manager, whom I called so that he could come and help out with the service. That is the advantage of living where you work. Most management lived on the island, a few meters away from the hotel.
- A waiter, who eventually showed up around 6 p.m. and also tired from New Year's Eve celebrations.
- A hostess, who was extremely helpful in arranging welcome drinks to slow down the flow of guests into the restaurant.

Well, that is a ratio of about 17 guests to one employee: to welcome, take drinks and food orders, serve drinks, prepare dishes, serve them, and so on.

We held on up until around after 50 guests were seated, then as more guests came in, we gradually started to lose the battle. In the end, quite miraculously, we somehow managed to feed every one of our guests, but luxury standards were not met that night for sure, and the consequences for the business were quite dramatic.

During service, I could see many hands raised everywhere across the restaurant; I had become the center of attraction for the evening, but for the wrong reason!! At that moment, I just was expecting to be lynched on the motu's highest coconut tree before the evening was over.

The morning after, as many guests were checking out, they, of course, wanted to have a last word with *the manager* ... 2002 was definitely starting in style!

Nevertheless, many years after, I still think Bora Bora is one of the most beautiful places on Earth, and its people are among the most genuine and warmest I have ever met.

This must be the main reason why guests from all over the world keep returning to French Polynesia: a true smile is, after all, as equally or even more important, than speedy and accurate service. As said earlier, luxury is not just about technicity and skills but also relies greatly on staff attitude and personality.

There is always something positive to learn, even with life's traumatic experiences, as they always point out at something valuable, which is not always obvious right away, but eventually becomes so. The lesson learned on this particular night is that, no matter how hard or difficult the task might seem to be, you have to give it your best and just get on with it, and think of the hundreds of guests attended in perfect conditions.

This is a common trait with hoteliers around the world; think about it next time you check in into a palace; behind the impeccable looks and smile, there is that man on a wire.

Figure 3.46 Beautiful Bora Bora Pearl Beach Resort, French Polynesia

Luxury hospitality's inside story: avoid a diplomatic incident, know your menu!

La Cumbre de Rio, organized in Peru and hosted in Cusco at the Hotel Monasterio, was a continuous stream of events in and out of the hotel: press conferences, meetings, bilateral presidential gatherings. Last-minute events, cancelations, changes of guest numbers were the norm, and the food and beverage teams were *on call* throughout the whole duration of the events, ready to attend to any new requirement.

Events could take place anywhere in the hotel: suites, gardens, patios, or the main lobby. The beautifully decorated *Capilla*, an original colonial era chapel, adjacent to the hotel's lobby, had been transformed in the Cumbre's headquarters, constantly hosting meetings with their cohorts of local and international journalists.

Figure 3.47 Hotel Monasterio's private chapel, used for many events, such as the Presidents' meetings during La Cumbre de Rio

Many functions were also held outside the hotel, on the many archeological sites in Cusco and its suburbs: Koricancha (also known as the Temple of the Sun), La Merced Convent, Sacsayhuaman (also locally known as *sexy woman*, a mnemotechnic helper for non-Spanish speakers), and many other very interesting historical sites.

In luxury food and beverage, it is the combination of literally thousands of details that will contribute to success. This constant attention to detail makes it very challenging, even more so when you are dealing with heads of states and ministers throughout the day. It can actually be a bit nerve-wracking at times!

On a particular morning, May 24, 9 a.m., the Capilla was hosting a high-profile gathering: the official opening ceremony of the Cumbre de Rio's session in Cusco.

Heads of states from 19 Latin America countries, together with their respective delegations, were gathered inside for a few hours, discussing the continent's future.

Meanwhile, the food and beverage team was working around the clock to make sure every single detail was taken care of. So, of course, on that day, everyone was onboard from very early in the morning to check and recheck lights, sound, temperature, chair height, cleanliness, flower arrangements, water bottles, pencils, cleanliness and alignment of glasses, and a hundred more details so that nothing could go wrong.

The presidents' group was made of about 50 guests, and they had a coffee break scheduled at 10:30 in the magnificent main patio of the hotel, meters away from the chapel's entrance.

A buffet had been set up for the occasion, adjacent to the chapel's outside wall. My food and beverage colleagues and I were all excited and nervous at the thought of having such important guests all gathered in one place; our performance for this first event had to be absolutely faultless!

So, there we were, checking and rechecking each detail over and over again, on and around the buffet: fresh fruit juices, coffee, varieties of teas, infusions, including the delicious local coca leaf tea, which is very efficient in preventing altitude sickness.

A standard in luxury food and beverage, when preparing a buffet or coffee break for a group, requires that everything must be ready 30 minutes before the event starts. It is a real important one, as it makes a huge difference to guest service; it just does not look professional if the waiters are struggling to complete the buffet until the very last minute.

Another simple reason is that guests might decide to start their coffee break a little earlier, and that is something that high-quality service needs to anticipate. That is what happened precisely on that memorable day, as the presidents and their respective entourages started to come out of the chapel 20 minutes ahead of schedule! They had been in the chapel for some time and were very much looking forward to coffee, pastries, and fruits; in a matter of minutes, they were taking over the whole buffet.

At that precise moment, I was busy stirring the freshly squeezed fruit juices, on the buffet's end corner, when I saw a large shadow hanging over me. I looked up and saw President Vicente Fox, Mexico's President at the time, making his way toward the juice section. He is a very tall man, and I will never forget his handshake, not only because you do not shake a president's hand on a regular basis, but because he has large hands and a firm grip!

Just after we had greeted, he reached for an empty glass, about to help himself with an orange-colored juice; was it orange? or papaya juice?? Both were on display, next to each other, but their labels were missing!

I had to act very fast, but I could not move easily, as I was cornered between the wall and the buffet. So, I mentally prepared myself and anticipated my answer to the question I knew was coming: "cuál es el jugo de papaya? (which one is the papaya juice?)"

Gathering all my self-confidence, and some useful experience in the field too, I pointed to the one on the left, and it turned out I was right, but that was a close call!

This story just shows that no matter how prepared you think you are, something may always happen: I found out later that the wind had blown off the labels from the table, as I found them later on, on the floor and just a couple a feet away from the buffet! It really helps to know every single detail of the food and beverage items that are displayed on the buffet or written on the menu. There is simply no valid excuse for not knowing!

Review questions

1. Which are the positions found in a kitchen brigade?
2. What are the characteristics of a French service? When is it used?
3. Why is the stewarding department so important within food and beverage?
4. Which are the differences between front and back of the house?
5. In the absence of an executive chef, who takes over the kitchen's responsibility?
6. What are the key positions within the food and beverage department?
7. Which are the main objectives of a food and beverage department?
8. What are the particularities of the banqueting department?
9. What are the advantages and disadvantages of buffets?
10. What are the main responsibilities of a food and beverage manager?

Exercises

- Choose a luxury hotel in your geographical area and list the various components of its food and beverage department.
- If possible, contact the person in charge of the department, to obtain further information such as: number of staff, key positions, concepts of restaurants, number of guests served, and so on.
- You are the food and beverage manager of a soon-to-be-opened luxury 250-room hotel located in the city center. You have been asked to develop the food and beverage offer based on the assumption that 70 percent of the future guests will stay at the property for leisure purposes, three nights on average.
  - Which outlets and food and beverage services would you propose?
  - Which staffing structure would be required for such a structure?

CHAPTER 4

Key Performance Indicators in Food and Beverage Management

In this chapter, the focus is on the *financial good health* indicators commonly used in food and beverage management.

While they are not the only tools used to assess of a healthy operation, they constitute an important measurement and are the basic tools used every day in food and beverage management.

Keywords				
Adjustments	Consumption	Indicators	Point of	System
Analysis	Cost	Inventory	sales (POS)	Transfers
Average check	Covers	Labor cost	Profit	Unit
Benchmark	Daily report	Margin	Purchases	Value
Budgeted	End of month	Methods	Ratio	Variable
Cost of goods	report	Net profit	Revenue	Variance
sold (COGS)	Expenses	Payroll	Return on	Volume
Consolidated	Forecast	Percentages	sales (ROS)	Wages
	Gross profit	Performance	Salaries	
	percentage	Period	Sales	
	Income		Statement	
			Stock	

Main Food and Beverage Indicators and Ratios

Food and Beverage Sales, Revenue, or Income

Food and beverage sales are, in most cases, calculated by a point of sales (POS) system, on a daily basis, and consolidated in monthly figures.

Such systems will also record the number of guests served, under the heading *covers*; a cover is equivalent to a guest. In operations that are not using electronic POS systems, such figures can be reported manually or using a cash register.

Number of covers

Knowing how many guests were attended to during the day is a very useful indicator of a business's health, in addition to the amount of sales that were achieved. In the food and beverage industry, it is common to consider covers as guests who consume a meal in the restaurant. A guest coming in for a coffee or lemonade or any other type of drink will generate sales but will not be recorded as a cover.

A bar or a nightclub, serving mostly drinks, would, on the other hand, consider each guest as a cover, as beverage is the main source of revenue.

Situational examples

Situation 1
Four guests have dinner at a restaurant. Pre-dinner drinks are served, as well as a bottle of wine with their meal: four food covers + four beverage covers are recorded.

Situation 2
As in Situation 1, the four guests sit down at a table together; however, only two of them consume meals, and all four have the same drinks as in situation 1: two food covers + four beverage covers are recorded in this case.

Situation 3
Four guests have cocktails at the bar, and one of them orders snacks: four beverage covers + one food cover are recorded.

These examples describe what is generally done in the industry; however, the way of recording covers may vary from organization to organization. The important thing is that a coherent and consistent recording system is put in place by management.

There is a good reason behind careful recording of the covers figures: they are the base for the calculation of the *average check*, another important ratio in food and beverage. As we will see later, the combination of covers and average checks allows the drafting of budgets and precise analysis of profit and loss statements.

Average check

The average check, also called average spent per customer, is a ratio used daily in restaurants: it informs the manager of the spending trend of customers. As mentioned earlier, the average food check of a fine-dining restaurant, such as a one Michelin star, is around 100 U.S. dollars per cover.

Now let us examine the mechanics of covers and average check ratios, the basis for any of the planning and analysis activities in food and beverage management:

Food average check

Total food sales/total food covers
Example:
Food sales: $24,200
Food covers: 450
Food average check: $24,200/450 = $53.77

Beverage average check

Total beverage sales/total beverage covers
Example:
Beverage sales: $4,500
Beverage covers: 520
Beverage average check: $4,500/520 = $8.65

Note that food and beverage average checks should first be calculated separately, in order to have useful and accurate measurements, which can be compared from day to day, month to month, and also on a yearly basis.

Food and Beverage Costs or Expenses

Categories of Expenses in Food and Beverage

Expenses, as opposed to sales or revenue, represent all the costs associated with the food and beverage operation. They are divided in four main sections:

Food cost
Beverage cost

Labor cost

Other expenses

Food cost, beverage cost, and labor cost are generally the highest costs generated by a food and beverage department. The three categories costs added together are called *prime cost*.

In the luxury segment, food and beverage costs are usually higher, as quality products are more often used than in other types of establishments. The cost of labor is also usually higher as more staff are required, with higher levels of skills. For example, salaries for a pastry chef, a sommelier, or a chief baker in a Michelin-starred restaurant may represent a large percentage of the food and beverage payroll.

Food and beverage costs may also be referred to as *COGS* (cost of goods sold)

STRUCTURE OF COSTS

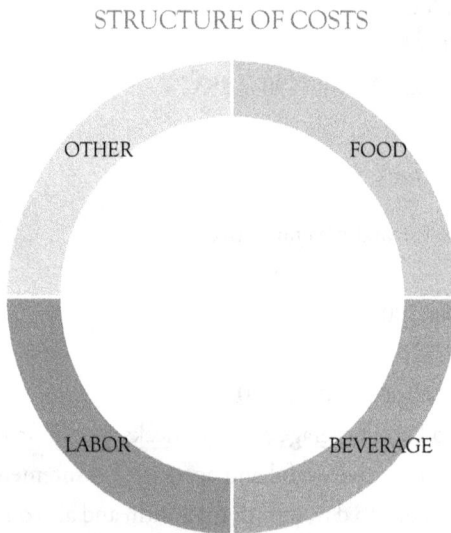

Figure 4.1 Cost repartition in the food and beverage department

Cost of Goods Sold (COGS)

Also referred to as *food cost* or *cost of food sales*, COGS is the main benchmark used in any food and beverage operation. Whenever chefs or food and beverage managers meet for a strategic budget meeting, or when reviewing end of the month results, COGS is the main indicator that will be taken into account.

This ratio is calculated at least once per month, by the financial department of the hotel, and is presented in the monthly profit and loss statement, or income statement, which will be further detailed in the following chapter.

As for the average check ratios, COGS should be calculated separately for food and beverage.

The food cost

The food cost is calculated by comparing the product consumption to the sales that were generated.

Obtaining restaurant sales is relatively easy with computerized systems in use today; however, finding out what the exact consumption is a little bit more complex, as most food sales are made of many different ingredients.

In this chapter, we will explore two methods of calculating food consumption: the inventory method and the daily food cost method.

The inventory method

Here is the formula used to calculate food consumption in a food and beverage outlet:

Beginning or opening inventory Computed the *first* day of the month, by counting or weighing all food products in the kitchen
➕
Issues to the kitchen Obtained by costing all food products transferred to the kitchen, from the hotel's general stores
➖
Ending inventory Computed the *last* day of the month, by counting or weighing all food products in the kitchen
＝
Total food consumed

Once the total food consumption is obtained, certain adjustments will have to be made, such as the cost of food that has been used to produce employees' meals, or product transfers to and from the outlet. Such transfers may be fruits transferred from the pastry to the bar for the making of cocktails or fresh juices, for example.

The value of employees' meals is usually predetermined by the human resources department, with the chef's assistance. If, for example, it costs 3.00 U.S. dollars to produce an employee meal per day, then this amount has to be deducted from the overall food cost. The reason for this is that employees' meals are considered, in accounting terms, as a staff benefit, and should therefore be allocated to human resources costs rather than food cost.

To be relevant, all food and beverage ratios, such as the COGS, should be expressed as a percentage of sales.

Example

Month end results	
Total sales	$750,000
Food sales	75% of total sales
Beverage sales	25% of total sales
Beginning food inventory	$25,000
Ending food inventory	$30,000
Total food issues	$200,000
Employee meal cost	$6,000
Transfers to bars	$250
Transfers from bars	$125

Calculation of food cost:

Food consumed: $25,000 + $200,000 = $225,000 − $30,000 = **$195,000**

COGS: $195,000 − $6,000 − $250 + $125 = **$188,875**

Total food sales: $750,000 * 75/100 = **$562,500**

Food cost %: $188,875/$562,500 * 100 = **33.6% (rounded to one digit)**

This result means that for every 100 U.S. dollars of revenue generated by food sales, the operator had to spend 33.60 U.S. dollars in food products. This is a percentage that may correspond to a fine-dining operation.

Food cost percentage is a very meaningful benchmark for any food and beverage operation, as it assesses its healthy management.

The food cost percentage should be compared both to the budgeted and the previous year's figures. This will be the main subject of the profit and loss statement section.

The daily food cost method

Counting inventories, also called stocktaking, can be timely, as every item needs to be counted or weighted individually. This task may take a few hours each month for large operations.

For certain establishments, this does not make business sense, as labor hours, which are often the costliest post in fine-dining operations, are best spent in the kitchen production.

Also, smaller restaurant operations tend to have limited storage space in the kitchen, and chefs will focus on the day's stock to increase the turnover and use the freshest possible food products. For these reasons, most of the stock is used in the daily production and replenished the next day. It is right to assume that on average, the value of inventory will not vary greatly from day to day, and therefore, the daily food cost method may be used.

This method will focus on the cost price of direct purchases, their amounts will be recorded on a daily basis, and consolidated throughout the month. The great advantage of this method is that, besides saving precious time, it also computes a daily figure, rather than a monthly one.

Another advantage for food and beverage management and the executive chef is that the daily inventory method indicates a cost trend, enabling a faster reaction from management if anything looks out of line compared to expectations.

Example

	Food purchases		Revenue		Food cost %		Staff food
	Daily	MTD*	Daily	MTD*			
Date	$	$	$	$	% day	% MTD*	$
1	3,782	3,782	11,513	11,513	32.85%	32.85%	-839
2	19,019	22,801	7,553	19,066	251.81%	119.59%	-839
3	-839	21,963	13,217	32,283	-6.35%	68.03%	-839
4	12,941	34,903	18,090	50,373	71.54%	69.29%	-839
5	-839	34,065	18,094	68,467	-4.64%	49.75%	-839
6	-839	33,226	19,418	87,885	-4.32%	37.81%	-839
7	-839	32,387	19,201	107,086	-4.37%	30.24%	-839
8	6,303	38,690	7,141	114,227	88.26%	33.87%	-839
9	-839	37,851	10,719	124,946	-7.82%	30.29%	-839

Figure 4.2 Daily food cost calculation
* Month to date

In this example, the value of each day's purchases is compared to the daily revenue (sales), and the food allocated to staff is deducted daily, providing a net cost of food sold.

The food cost resulting is shown in the two *food cost* columns on the right. The *% day* column is not so relevant, as the kitchen may purchase ingredients in preparation for events taking place later in the week. For example, a banquet for 100 guests will be prepared over the course of several days, creating an off balance: for a few days, the cost of purchased ingredients will not be offset by any corresponding sale, as it will only be recorded on the day of the event. Therefore, the *% MTD* column, which shows the evolution throughout the month, is the most important one and needs to be monitored on a daily basis.

The first five to seven days of the month may not reveal much relevant information either, as it is typically a time when kitchens will restock. After this period, the cumulative food cost tends to stabilize and indicates the trend for the month. In the preceding example, we could expect a month end result of between 31 and 33 percent, corresponding to a fine-dining outlet.

The Beverage Cost

The beverage cost may be calculated using the food cost methods, although the staff transfers would not apply in this case.

Beverage cost for luxury operations tends to be, on average, between 20 and 25 percent. The percentage greatly depends on the wine list's references: the more luxury products are offered, the higher the cost percentage will tend to be.

There are many different levels of costs among beverage: mineral water, soft drinks, and coffee are usually the most profitable products, while high-quality wines, vintage champagnes, or cognacs have a much higher beverage cost.

Following on the previous example in the food cost section, let us now calculate the beverage cost according to the restaurant's sales and using the inventory method.

Example

Month end results	
Total sales	$750,000
Food sales	75% of total sales
Beverage sales	25% of total sales
Beginning beverage inventory	$5,000
Ending beverage inventory	$7,000
Total beverage issues	$35,000
Transfers to kitchens	$150
Transfers from kitchens	$135

Calculation of beverage cost:
Beverage consumed: $5,000 + $35,000 = $40,000 – $7,000 = **$33,000**
COGS: $33,000 – $150 + $135 = **$32,985**
Total beverage sales: $750,000 * 25/100 = **$187,500**
Beverage cost %: $32,985/$187,500 * 100 = 17.6% (**rounded to one digit**)

This result means that for every 100 U.S. dollars of revenue generated by beverage sales, the operator had to spend 17.60 U.S. dollars in beverage products, in line with the expected spending of a fine-dining operation.

As for the food cost percentage, the beverage cost should be compared both to the budgeted, and the previous year's figures.

Review questions

1. What are the main ratios measuring the food and beverage department's efficiency?
2. Why are inventories necessary?
3. Is staff food included in *COGS*?
4. What is an *average check*?
5. Who is responsible for the COGS?
6. What are the benefits of using the *daily food cost* technique?
7. Which are food and beverage's greatest expenses?
8. What is a *cover*? When is it used?
9. What are examples of transfers to bars?
10. When are inventories required?

Exercises

Calculate the food cost, in value and percentage, using the inventory method:

Food cost calculation—inventory method			
Inventory January 31			$21,580
February purchases:			
Meat		$10,420	
Dairy		$3,201	
Fruits and vegetables		$4,320	
Dry goods		$15,320	

Food cost calculation—inventory method			
Total purchases			
Number of employees eating daily	50		
Cost per employee meal	$3.00		
Inventory on April 30			$19,530
Beginning inventory			
Purchases			
Goods available for sale			
Ending inventory			
Cost of food consumed			
Employee meals (30 days)			
Cost of food sold			
Food revenue February	$65,450		
Food cost % February			

Complete the daily food cost report for the first week of January, comment on the trends observed in the food cost evolution.

DAILY FOOD COST REPORT

			TODAY					TODATE		
DATE	DAY	OPENING FOOD STORE ROOM INVENTORY	FOOD PURCHASES	TOTAL FOOD AVAILABLE	FOOD REQUISITIONS	FOOD SALES	FOOD COST	FOOD PURCHASES	FOOD REQUISITIONS	FOOD SALES	FOOD COST
JAN		$	$	$	$	$	%	$	$	$	%
1	M	1537	321	1858	290	1243	23,33%	321	290	1243	
2	T		385	1953	370	980	37,76%	706	660		29,69%
3	W	1583	404		440	1100	40,00%	1110	1100	3323	33,10%
4	T	1547	480	2027	480	1050		1590	1580	4373	36,13%
5	F	1547	890	2437	405	1005	40,30%	2480	1985	5378	36,91%
6	S	2032	203	2235	535	1490	35,91%		2520	6868	
	TOTALS										

The Profit and Loss Statement

Main Objectives

The profit and loss, commonly called P&L statement, provides a detailed analysis of the volume of sales, the food and beverage expenses, labor expenses and other expenses. It also indicates the level of profitability, or loss, when expenses exceed revenue, of an outlet or department.

Also named the income statement, is it computed at least once a month, after all inventories and sales have been reconciled. The financial department prepares this document, which is based on the information collected in the kitchens and food and beverage outlets. It is extremely important for any food and beverage manager or executive chef to be able to analyze and interpret this report.

The profit and loss statement is similar to a thermometer; it provides management with a clear picture of the business's health and indicates the efficiency of an operation. The profit and loss statement is analyzed regularly and is a good base to suggest action plans or implement new food and beverage control procedures for future improvement.

It is also worth noting that most staff holding management positions in the food and beverage department, particularly so in international luxury hotel chains, are regularly evaluated on their ability to meet established profit and loss targets.

The profit and loss statement contains six critical operational areas:

- Volume of sales
- Food cost
- Beverage cost
- Labor cost
- Other expenses, broken down in controllable and non-controllable expenses
- Profit or loss

As stated in the previous section, the greatest expenses in a high-level food and beverage operation are food and beverage costs and labor costs, or the *prime cost*.

The profit and loss statement allows a detailed analysis of the prime cost, as well as the other expenses incurred by food and beverage sales activities. Corporate food and beverage managers or executive chefs, in charge of multiple units, may receive profit and loss comparative data from district or regional managers and establish performance ratings among the various unit managers for each city, region, state, or nation.

Month to date						
Last year	%	Budget	%	Actual	%	Description
						Revenue
159,691	79.3	165,247	75.7	381,948	100.6	Food
16,412	8.2	14,581	6.7	53,681	14.1	Beverage
31,405	15.6	38,575	17.7	62,956	16.6	Other income
207,508	103.1	218,402	100.0	498,586	131.3	Subtotal revenue
(6,187)	(3.87)	-	-	(6,814)	(1.78)	Less rebated food
-	-	-	-	-	-	Less rebated beverage
-	-	-	-	(112,013)	(177.92)	Less rebated others
201,321	100.0	218,402	100.0	379,760	100.0	Total revenue
						Cost of sales
45,082	29.37	49,244	29.80	27,605	7.36	Food cost
666	4.06	2,041	14.00	5,951	11.09	Beverage cost
45,749	22.7	51,285	23.5	33,556	8.8	Total cost of sales
						Payroll and related expenses
40,302	20.0	75,611	34.6	48,632	12.8	Salaries and wages
40,302	20.0	75,611	34.6	48,632	12.8	Subtotal
21,514	10.7	17,156	7.9	20,700	5.5	Employee benefits
6,116	3.0	16,709	7.7	12,060	3.2	Service charge
67,932	33.7	109,476	50.1	81,391	21.4	Total payroll and related expenses
						Other expenses
2,483	1.2	1,586	0.7	3,115	0.8	Laundry and valet
24,517	12.2	7,674	3.5	26,822	7.1	Casual worker
3,000	1.5	358	0.2	705	0.2	Guest supplies
-	-	307	0.1	469	0.1	Cleaning supplies
1,177	0.6	1,535	0.7	1,927	0.5	Printing and stationery
60	0.0	1,023	0.5	35,179	9.3	Decorations
7,434	3.7	2,967	1.4	13,454	3.5	Operating expenses
-	-	-	-	-	-	Postage
1,978	1.0	1,739	0.8	3,917	1.0	Kitchen fuel
-	-	460	0.2	230	0.1	Music and entertainment

Month to date						
Last year	%	Budget	%	Actual	%	Description
-	-	51	0.0	-	-	Menu lists
623	0.3	409	0.2	629	0.2	Telephone
-	-	-	-	-	-	Promotion
150	0.1	205	0.1	73,112	19.3	Other expenses
41,421	20.6	18,315	8.4	159,560	42.0	Total other expenses
155,102	77.0	179,076	82.0	274,507	72.3	Total cost and expenses
46,218	23.0	39,326	18.0	105,253	27.7	Total banquet profit/(loss)
4,000		5,116		12,643		Covers
38,38		32,30		29,67		Food average check/cover
4,10		2,85		4,25		Beverage average check/cover

Figure 4.3 Profit and loss statement

Profit Calculation

There are two main levels of profit calculation for a food and beverage operation:

- The gross operating profit (GOP)
- The net profit, or net income

The gross operating profit

This indicator is useful in assessing the efficiency of an operation, concentrating on product consumption only. It is a benchmark, which can be easily compared between different business units within a chain for example.

The GOP is obtained by the following formula:

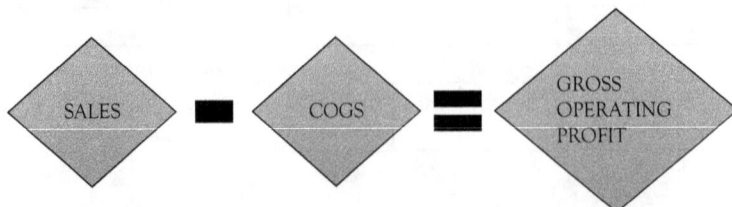

Example

For the month of January (in $):

Food sales	45,500
Beverage sales	12,300
Food cost	13,500
Beverage cost	3,250
Labor cost	19,500
Other expenses	6,200

Revenue	January	%
Food	45,500	78.7
Beverage	12,300	21.3
Total	57,800	100
Cost of sales		
Food	13,500	29.7
Beverage	3,250	26.4
Total	16,750	29
GOP		
Food	32,000	70.3
Beverage	9,050	73.6
Total	41,050	71

Net Profit or Income

To calculate net profit, all expenses have to be deducted from the GOP.
They are, in order of importance:

- Labor cost
- Other expenses

Using the preceding example, here are the month's results:

Revenue	January	%
Food	45,500	78.7
Beverage	12,300	21.3
Total revenue	57,800	100
Cost of sales		
Food	13,500	29.7
Beverage	3,250	26.4
Total cost of sales	16,750	29
GOP		
Food	32,000	70.3
Beverage	9,050	73.6
Total GOP	41,050	71
Labor cost	19,500	33.7
Other expenses	6,200	10.7
Net profit or loss	15,350	26.6

The result shows a profitability percentage of 26.6, meaning that for every 100 U.S. dollars of food and beverage sales, the business has generated 26.60 U.S. dollars of profit. This is an example of a healthy and well-managed food and beverage venture.

The formula for profit calculation is as follows:

Revenue, 100%

- Food and beverage cost %

- Labor cost %

- Other expense %

= Profit or loss %

Example

During the month of January, Restaurant Blue Oyster achieved food sales of

$8,600, and after inventories, recorded the following costs:

Food cost	$2,354
Labor cost	$1,892
Other expenses	$1,720

GOP: $8,600 – $2,354 = $6,246, or 72.6% of sales

Net profit: $6,246 – $1,892 – $ 1,720 = $2,634 or 30.6% of sales

Profit and Loss Statement Analysis

The primary objective of a food and beverage profit and loss statement is to provide relevant and useful information for the main stakeholders involved in any commercial venture:

- Management
- Shareholders
- Owners
- Creditors

It analyzes strategic information such as:

- Amount of sales
- How much money was spent to realize those sales?
- How much profit was made at the end of the period?

Analysis of the Volume of Sales

The analysis procedure of each of these areas can be divided in three main steps:

- Determine sales for the period, usually corresponding to one month
- Compare this figure to budgeted or targeted sales and proceed to calculate the difference between the two figures
- Express this difference in percentage, in relation with the budgeted sales

Such analysis may highlight different scenarios:

- Similar number of covers were served, at a higher average check
- More guests than targeted were served, at a similar than budgeted average check
- More guests served, at a higher average check
- Fewer guests served, at a higher average check
- And so on.

Expense Analysis

When analyzing expenses, the first instinctive reaction would be to wish for the lowest possible expenses, and therefore, the highest possible profit. In luxury operations, that approach may be lead to lack of quality in the products offered to guests.

So, let us look closely at the following statement: *low* costs are good and *high* costs are bad. It will only depend on what the primary expectation is, or in other words, what was planned, or budgeted for.

Let us take an example: the food cost has decreased by 5 percent between April and May, how could this be interpreted? It could be that the costs were better managed than previously, but it could also very well mean that the portions served were smaller than they should have been, or that the standard of quality of products was lowered. In both cases, it is clearly detrimental for the guest.

Of course, high costs should be avoided as well, in order not to run the risk of generating losses. However, overcontrolling costs at the expense of guest service will result in a series of issues, ranging from guest complaints, or number of covers decreasing, negative comments on social media, to name a few.

So, the trick is to find the right balance, keeping in mind that most improvements in business operations, provided they are carefully planned and assessed, should yield more customers, which, in turn, will yield greater operational expense. All costs are not necessarily negative, they just need to be monitored and controlled, hence the need to forecast expenses ahead.

Labor or Staff Cost

This expense includes all salaries, wages, and benefits such as food, laundry, accommodation, if any, and any other expense that is related to staff. For example, when hiring a restaurant manager for a fine-dining outlet, the cost of his or her transportation to get to the place of interview may be charged to labor cost.

In most food and beverage operations, staff costs are considered a fixed cost, because for the most part, monthly salaries are paid. Although, from time to time, there are variable costs that are added to the overall payroll cost of salaries and wages. The most common example is in the banqueting department, as the remuneration of part-time waiters or waitresses for a large banquet is a variable expense.

When total sales volume increases, fixed labor cost percentages will decline. On the contrary, variable labor costs will increase along with the volume of sales. As with food and beverage costs, COGS, staff expenses provide a number of useful productivity ratios.

The general productivity ratio, which is mostly used in the industry, is the labor cost percentage, which simply compares the total labor costs, fixed and variable, to the food and beverage sales.

The benchmark will vary greatly, depending on the type of establishment, the number of employees, and of course, the geographical location. For example, in Europe, a fine-dining restaurant may have a labor cost of around 40 percent, making it the greatest expense on the profit and loss statement.

$$ \text{Cost of Labor} \div \text{Total Sales} = \text{Labor Cost \%} $$

The cost of labor will always appear in the profit and loss statement, following the COGS ratio.

Other interesting ratios may be added to the profit and loss report, in the form of statistics, such as:

- Labor U.S. dollars spent per guest served
- Guests served per labor hour
- RevPASH, or revenue per available seat hour

Depending on the needs of the operation, any or all of these ratios can be used.

Let us have a look at them one by one in more detail:

Labor U.S. dollars spent per guest served

Week	Labor cost U.S. dollars	Guest served	Labor U.S. dollars spent per guest
1	6,500	875	7.42
2	9,030	1,138	7.93
3	8,543	1,024	8.34
4	6,327	698	9.06
TOTAL	30,400	3,735	8.13

This ratio expresses the cost of labor for each guest served, giving a more precise indication of productivity than the overall labor cost percentage. It is very useful for budgeting purpose when the manager needs to follow the year to year evolution.

Restaurant operators, wishing to compare performance among different outlets, would also gain valued information from such a ratio.

Guests served per labor hour

Week	Guests served	Labor hours used	Guest served per labor hour
1	740	663	1.11
2	850	648	1.31
3	1,242	850	1.46
4	992	790	1.25
TOTAL	3,824	2,951	1.29

This ratio is very useful for measuring productivity. It is mostly used in high-volume restaurant operations, where many diners are served simultaneously, such as a fast food or cafeteria for example.

It would probably not be used in a fine-dining restaurant, where guests tend to seat for a longer time.

Revenue per available seat hour (RevPASH)

This ratio evaluates how much guests spend. It also gives information on the speed of service, or table rotation, as well as an occupancy rate of the dining room.

Time slot	Seats available	Guests served	Sales ($)	RevPASH ($)
7–8 pm	50	25	500	10
8–9 pm	50	40	1,250	25
9–10 pm	50	50	2,000	40
Total	150	115	3,750	25
Seat occupancy	115/150 = 76.7%			

RevPASH is useful for high-volume restaurants, where seat rotation is frequent, for example, fast-food operations and coffee shops.

Profit Analysis

The profit margin represents the amount of profit generated on each U.S. dollars of sales, it is that portion of a U.S. dollar sale returned to the operation in the form of profits. Profit margin is also known as return on sales, or ROS. This ratio can also be used to evaluate a manager's overall effectiveness.

Profit margin percentage is calculated using the following formula:

A positive ROS provides a profit, and a negative profit will mean the company generated a loss, or that expenses were greater than sales.

An operation's profit variance percentage for an accounting period is measured by the following formula:

$$\frac{\text{Net Income This Period} - \text{Net Income Last Period}}{\text{Net Income Last Period}} = \text{Profit Variance \%}$$

Review questions

1. What are food and beverage's greatest expenses?
2. Which are the various ways of presenting labor ratios?
3. Is a high food cost necessarily a negative sign?
4. What does ROS mean?
5. Why is it useful to determine the average check?
6. How often should a profit and loss statement be computed?
7. Which sections are highlighted in the profit and loss statement?
8. What is the meaning of GOP?
9. What is included in *prime cost*?
10. Is the RevPASH method useful for a three Michelin star restaurant?

Exercises

Gross profit
Calculate the outlet's gross profit

Blue Bayou restaurant (in U.S. dollars)		
	This year	**%**
Sales		
Food	2,675,889	73.5%
Beverage	965,660	26.5%
Total sales	3,641,549	100.0%
Cost of sales		

Blue Bayou restaurant (in U.S. dollars)		
	This year	**%**
Food	1,074,420	40.2%
Beverage	115,879	12.0%
Total cost of sales	1,190,299	32.7%
Gross profit		
Food		
Beverage		
Total gross profit		

Percentages, net profit

Calculate the relevant percentages, as well as restaurant's profits

Blueberry Hill Restaurant (in U.S. dollars)				
	This year	**%**	**Last year**	**%**
Sales	1,020,064		954,030	
Expenses	703,045		695,088	
Profit				

RevPASH and seat occupancy

Calculate Blue Bayou restaurant's RevPASH, as well as seat occupancy for the period

Date: Thursday, November 24, 2019

Time slot	Seats available	Guests served	Sales (U.S. dollars)	REVPASH (U.S. dollars)
3–4 pm	0	0	0	
4–5 pm	75	5	154	
5–6 pm	75	12	386	
6–7 pm	75	25	850	
7–8 pm	75	60	1,872	
8–9 pm	75	45	1,690	
9–10 pm	75	38	1,245	
10–11 pm	75	11	478	
11–12 pm	0	0	0	
Total				
Seat occupancy				

CHAPTER 5

Food and Beverage Cost Control

Keywords			
Actual cost	Departmentalization	Non-controllable	Sales
Amount	Estimates	expenses	Security
Attainable cost	Expenditure	Other expenses	concerns
Audit	Expense	Perishability	Spoilage
Benchmark	Fixed costs	Potential cost of	Standardized
Breakage	Food and beverage	sales	recipes
Classification	cost control	Profitability	Theft
Comparison	Ingredients	Purchasing	Theoretical
Control	Inventories	Random	inventory
Controllable	Management	inventories	Variable
expenses	Menu	Ratio	costs
Controller	Mixed expenses	Recipe cost cards	Volume
		Revenue control	Waste

This chapter explores the various methods of controlling costs in the food and beverage department. Tools such as standard recipes, portion sizes, attainable and actual food costs comparison are exposed, in order for the reader to familiarize with the basic operating ratios used in food and beverage management.

Food and beverage cost control spans over all the operational phases of food and beverage: from purchasing to revenue collection, its ultimate goal is to ensure that all product purchased is sold.

Food and Beverage Cost Control Processes

Generally speaking, the cost control process may be broken down in three main phases:

- *The planning phase:* which characterizes most of management's activities, for example, elaborating policies, standards, or determining departmental objectives.
- *The operational phase:* performed by managers, heads of department, and supervisors; it consists in the day-to-day control activities within the food and beverage department, from purchasing to customer service and revenue collection.
- *The post-operational phase:* day-to-day control of activities performed by the food and beverage cost control department, which is generally an entity reporting directly to the financial director. The post-operational phase is a second layer of control, during which the food and beverage controller will randomly audit the control systems carried out by food and beverage management. For example, the food and beverage controller may organize random inventories in order to assess food or beverage cost of sales.

The objective of this chapter is to detail the operational phase, in order to ensure there are as few as possible differences between the quantity of products purchased and the finished products that are eventually sold to the customer.

This is particularly challenging in food and beverage, as most items sold to the customer are made of many products, which will undergo many transformations during the operational process. For example, a dish on the à la carte menu may easily contain 20 to 30 different ingredients. In addition to this, fine-dining restaurants use a lot of raw products, generating wastage such as peels, bones, skin, and so on, which needs to be recorded as well in order to obtain the true potential cost of producing a recipe.

To overcome these challenges, a number of processes should be put in place. The sum of such processes is referred to as a *food and beverage cost control system.* Various management tools will be detailed in this section:

- Analysis of income and expenditure
- Creation and update of recipe cost cards
- Calculation of standard costs and potential profitability
- Comparison of actual costs with attainable costs

However, because of the nature of a food and beverage operation, there will always be a degree of product waste or spoilage, due to the perishability of most ingredients used.

Other potential threats are product misuse, for example, when a high-quality ingredient is used to prepare a lower-cost preparation.

Unfortunately, there are numerous cases of discrepancies in the industry that are also related to breakage or theft. The next section outlines the main concerns and specific challenges encountered by operators in the industry.

Specific Challenges to Food and Beverage Cost Control

Perishability

On average, between 70 and 80 percent of the products used in a restaurant are perishable, which means their shelf life is of two to three days maximum. Without careful quantity planning, or lack of staff training, there is a high risk of product spoilage.

Business Volume Unpredictability

The volume of business each day and for each meal in food and beverage is by definition unpredictable. This is probably the food and beverage operator's greatest challenge, as even with the best forecasts, it is hard to predict how many customers will walk into the restaurant on a given day.

Menu Mix Unpredictability

Along with the unpredictability of business volumes, the menu mix is also hard to predict ahead of time. Not only is there a difficulty in predicting the number of guests for a service, it is hard to pinpoint with precision which dishes will be sold during a given service. Experience and menu analysis can help offset this challenge, up to a point.

Food and Beverage Operation Short Cycle

Food and beverage operations are characterized by a very short operation cycle. In a restaurant, unlike any other type of business, demand is generated by the customer at a definite moment and is instantly followed by production. Many actors of the front and back of the house are involved simultaneously, in a very limited period of time. All these factors make it a necessity to establish a tight control system of all food and beverage-related operations.

Departmentalization

Another trait of a food and beverage operation is that it is made of, and relies on, many departments. As described in the previous topics, the food and beverage guest cycle involves many actors, each one of them playing a specific role: the purchasing department procures goods, which are then stored in different outlets, and later transformed by the kitchen(s). Front of the house team delivers the end products to the customer and collects the revenue from the same. Should one actor malfunction, this will have an immediate effect on the guest experience, as all the departments are closely related and dependent on each other. Let us just imagine the purchasing department buys the wrong quantity of an ingredient, the kitchen production would then be affected and chefs would not be able to prepare a scheduled banquet on time. This would most likely lead to a guest complaint, affecting the business as a whole.

Security Concerns in the Food and Beverage Department

One basic rule of food and beverage control is that trust does not exclude control. As seen in the previous section, there are many transactions held every day within a food and beverage department, raising the risks of waste, spoilage, or theft.

Recent studies by the National Restaurant Association estimate that about 40 billion U.S. dollars are stolen yearly by employees in the restaurant industry.[1] These thefts are estimated to cause one-third of bank-ruptcies in the sector! According to the same study, theft costs estimates are of about 218 U.S. dollars per employee per year. The 20/20/60 rule applies to theft: 20 percent of employees would never steal anything from the company, 20 percent systematically would and 60 percent would if given the right opportunity and if they were confident they would not be blamed for it.[2]

Following are some examples of the most commonly used theft or embezzlement *techniques* in the hospitality sector.

Kickbacks

A kickback, also known as *under the table* commission, consists of an illegal rebate or gift given by a supplier to a buyer, in exchange for exclusive purchase from the supplier.

Short Orders and Incomplete Shipments

Deliveries that miss some of the items ordered by the buyer; this may be unintentional or intentional.

Inventory Theft (Shrinkage) and Inventory Substitutions

Theft from the inventory, occurs frequently, for example, from the kitchen fridges or in the wine cellar. The variety of goods available in a food and beverage operation makes it rather easy for anyone with the wrong intentions to remove stock for personal consumption or resale.

No Segregation in Operating Activities

It is vital for a hotel or restaurant to separate buying, receiving, storing, and bill paying procedures, in order to avoid breaches in the food and beverage control system. For example, the purchasing manager should be

---

[1] https://ahlei.org/product/managing-service-in-food-and-beverage-operations-fifth-edition-digital/

[2] https://ahlei.org/product/managing-service-in-food-and-beverage-operations-fifth-edition-digital/

responsible for food orders to suppliers, but invoices should be paid out by the financial control department, and goods quality should be checked by the executive chef or the food and beverage manager when they are delivered to the hotel. These practices allow cross-control and prevent any wrongdoing and errors.

Effective Methods and Recommendations to Prevent Security Concerns

There are many ways and methods that can be put in place to prevent most security concerns. Although there is no magic recipe to solve all security concerns, a set of minimum basic controls should be set in order to limit them as much as possible. Each method will have to be assessed by the operator in terms of efficiency and according to the particularities of the food and beverage operation.

Following are the industry's best practices, recommended for any food and beverage operation:

- Separate buying and paying activities.
- Organize independent, surprise external audits.
- Randomly inspect facilities, such as general stores, fridges, bars, or wine cellars.
- Random physical inventories should be conducted regularly, in all outlets and kitchens.
- Restrict access to high-cost products, for example, expensive cognac bottles should be kept in a locked cabinet.
- Conduct a critical item inventory value daily. Critical items are high-cost items, such as meat, seafood, certain wines, liquors, and so on.
- Staff background checks and reference checks should be carried out before any recruitment, by the human resources department.
- Lockers inspection should be organized randomly by the security and human resources departments, on a regular basis.
- Key control: a coherent and well-managed key system should be in place throughout the hotel. For example, after-hours

access to food and beverage stock should only be permitted to the hotel's duty manager, in presence of a member of security.

- CCTV and webcams should be installed in areas of the hotel that may be prone to theft, such as the staff's entrance, or the wine cellar for example.
- All employees' access to the premises should be screened by the security department.

The next section will be dedicated to the fundamental tools of control in the food and beverage department.

The Food Cost of Sales

Potential, Attainable or Theoretical Cost of Sales

As described in the key performance indicators of the food and beverage chapter, the food cost percentage is calculated using the formula:

$$\frac{\text{Cost of food sold}}{\text{Food Sales}} = \text{Food Cost \%}$$

As this method uses information based on daily or monthly inventories, it is considered to be the *real* figure, referred to as the *actual food cost*.

In order to be able to measure performance, the actual food cost figure needs to be regularly compared to a benchmark; for this reason, the potential, or attainable food cost needs, to be calculated.

As many ingredients make up a recipe, calculating the potential cost will require drafting recipe costing sheets, or standardized recipes.

Recipe Costing Sheets

This document is usually compiled by the executive chef and approved by the food and beverage manager. It is a great benchmarking tool, providing quantity and quality control of food and beverage products used in the various recipes. As such, it constitutes the basis of food and beverage control: for the manager or the owner of a business, it answers the questions "how much does this dish cost?" and "how much should I sell it in order to obtain a certain profitability?"

Recipe sheets are also useful for the purchasing department, as they will help the quantities of ingredients that need to be purchased.

Furthermore, it is used as a training tool for new staff in the kitchen, or in the bar, where many cocktails are made following recipe costing sheets.

NAME OF THE ARTICLE:			Dark Cocolate Mousse Tart	OUTLET:		MONTH :	
				By:		YEAR :	
QTY.	UOM		INGREDIENTS	SPECIFICATION	UNIT COST €	VALUE €
12	u	1	Egg Yolk	Organic B	0,294	3,53
0,25	kg	1	Sugar		0,67	0,17
0,4	kg	1	Dark Chocolate	alhrona 77% Guaran	29,00	11,60
0,35	l	1	Whipped Cream		6,96	2,44
0,09	l	1	Cognac	Courvoisier VSOP	27,00	2,43
0,2	l	1	Fresh Cream	Elle & Vire 40%	6,96	1,39
0,3	l	1	Whipped Cream	Elle & Vire 40%	6,96	2,09
0,175	kg	1	Flour		1,89	0,33
10	g	1000	Natural vanilla	Tahaa Iorana	89,02	0,89
1	g	10	Golden leaf		15,00	1,50
METHOD							

1 - Make Sabayon by whisking egg yolks and sugar.
2 - Boil the fresh cream and add the dark chocolate ' make truffle '
3 - Add the Cognac
4 - Add the whipped cream and all the the rest of the ingredients and mix well.
5 - Put a sponge base into the mould, add the chocolate mixture and chill in the refrigerator
6 - Dessert plate 21cm V&B, garnish with golden leaf

COST PRICE PER PORTION	2,64	COST	26,36
SUGGESTED SELLING PRICE PER PORTION	10,91		
COST %	24,16%	TOTAL COST	26,36
APPROVED SELLING PRICE PER PORTION	10,91	GROSS S/P	10,91
COST %	24,16%	V.A.T	1,09
PROFIT PER PORTION	8,27	NET S/P	12,00
PROFIT %	75,84%		
NO OF PORTION	10		
COMMENTS			
CAPACITY /WEIGHT /SIZE PER PORTION			

COST CALCULATED BY			
	COST CONTROLLER	EXECUTIVE CHEF	F&B MANAGER
UOM = UNIT OF MEASURE			

Figure 5.1 Recipe costing sheet

The cost obtained by adding up all the ingredients' values together is called the attainable or potential or theoretical cost. It is the cost of sales that would be achieved in absolutely ideal conditions, which of course never occurs in a kitchen environment: quantities are not always absolutely accurate to the gram, some liquid can be spilt, a piece of meat burnt, and so on.

Comparing Attainable and Actual Cost of Sales

Once the lengthy but necessary task of compiling all recipe sheets has been completed, the next step is to calculate the overall attainable cost of sales, which will be based on the number of dishes served.

Example

Menu item	Number of units sold	Portion Attainable cost (U.S. dollars)	Portion Sales price (U.S. dollars)	Total Attainable cost (U.S. dollars)	Total Sales price (U.S. dollars)
A	25	2.50	8.20	62.50	205,00
B	15	3.62	9.40	54.30	141,00
C	6	3.85	10.50	23.10	63,00
D	18	4.03	11.50	72.54	207,00
TOTAL				212.44	616.00

In the chart above, the total attainable cost of sales is 212.44 U.S. dollars, compared to sales of 616.00 U.S. dollars. Therefore, the *attainable % of cost of sales* is 34.5% (212.44 * 100/616.00).

This figure should be compared with the *actual food cost %,* found after analyzing inventories. Any variance of over 1.5 to 2 percent should be considered important and be further investigated by the executive chef, the food and beverage cost controller, and the food and beverage manager.

This control process should enable the executive chef and food and beverage manager answer vital management questions, such as:

• What is the difference between attainable and actual product costs?
• Are those differences acceptable?
• How close are we to our cost goals?

Cost of Sales Reduction

In order to achieve product costs and to reduce the gap between the attainable and actual costs, there are a number of cost control best practices in the industry, which are listed in the following chart:

| Best practices for cost of sales reduction ||
Food	Beverage
Minimize product loss by securing fridges in kitchen and general stores	A control system of in room minibars is in place
Management approval for all food transfers and issues	All banquet operations involving alcoholic drinks are carefully supervised, by a member of the food and beverage management team
No food product may be prepared without a docket from the waiter or waitress	Bar supervision is reinforced to avoid orders not being rung up or products to be substituted
All food received from suppliers is checked and signed for, by the purchasing manager and/or the chef	Requisitions and issues from general stores to bars and wine cellars are carefully monitored by management
Systematic inventories of all costly items are carried out by management	Mystery guests may be used from time to time
Recipe costings are reviewed regularly for accuracy, by the executive chef and the food and beverage controller	Random inventories are carried out regularly

Food and Beverage Other Expenses

Other expenses are all the cost of items that are neither food, beverage, nor labor.

These expenses can account for a significant amount of the total cost of operations. Other expenses can constitute almost anything in the food-service business, from toothpicks to piano rental or energy costs. Each operation will have its own unique list of required other expenses, for example, a seaside resort may need to use insect repellent on the beach to allow trouble-free dining. The cost of the insecticide would be allocated to the food and beverage department's profit and loss, under the heading *other expenses*.

In this section, we will have a look at the most current categories of other expenses.

Classification of Other Expenses

Controllable and Non-Controllable Expenses

Other expenses are classified in two subcategories: *controllable* and *non-controllable* expenses.

Certain expenses can be classified as both controllable and non-controllable. For example, in *Repairs and maintenance*, we may find maintenance contracts, which are payable on a monthly basis, and a one-off payment for spare parts for a walk-in fridge or a dishwasher in the kitchen. The monthly contracts would be controllable, with the one-off payment for the spare parts and non-controllable.

Most common controllable expenses
Music and entertainment
Marketing
Utilities: electricity, gas, water, garbage removal
General and administrative expenses (A&G)
Repairs and maintenance

Most common non-controllable expenses
Occupancy costs, such as rent
Equipment rental
Management fees
Interest on bank loans

Fixed, variable, or mixed expenses

Another common way of analyzing food and beverage other expenses is by determining whether they are fixed, variable, or mixed expenses.

A *fixed expense* is one that remains constant, despite increases or decreases in sales volume, such as rent, which is usually paid monthly.

Month	Fixed rent (U.S. dollars)	Revenue (U.S. dollars)	Rent %
January	4,000	54,000	7.40
February	4,000	61,000	6.56
March	4,000	72,000	5.56
April	4,000	24,500	16.32
May	4,000	36,300	11.01
June	4,000	70,000	5.71
Average	4,000	52,967	7.55

Other Expenses ÷ Total Sales = Other Expense Cost %

In this case, the rent percentage will vary with the sales volume; as they increase, the rental takes a less important part in the expenses, and its percentage decreases. On the other hand, if the sales level is lower than expected, the fixed amount allocated to rent will represent a higher percentage of expenses.

A *variable expense* is one that generally increases as sales volume increases and decreases as sales volume decreases.

Month	Sales (U.S. dollars)	Casual labor (%)	Casual labor (U.S. dollars)
January	95,000	7.00	6,650
February	97,500	7.00	6,825
March	103,500	7.00	7,245
April	122,000	7.00	8,540
May	148,000	7.00	10,360
June	132,000	7.00	9,240
Average	116,333	7.00	8,143

A *mixed expense* is one that has properties of both fixed and variable expenses.

Month	Sales (U.S. dollars)	Fixed labor cost (U.S. dollars)	Variable labor cost 1%	Labor expense (U.S. dollars)
January	95,000	4,000	950	4,950
February	97,500	4,000	975	4,975
March	103,500	4,000	1,035	5,035
April	122,000	4,000	1,220	5,220
May	148,000	4,000	1,480	5,480
June	132,000	4,000	1,320	5,320
Average	116,333	4,000	1,163	5,163

In summary,

Expense type	% of sales	U.S. dollars amount
Fixed	Decreases	Does not change
Variable	Does not change	Increases
Mixed	Decreases	Increases

Monitoring other expenses will require various assessment tools, such as calculating the ratio of expenses compared to the total sales in food and beverage.

Other Expense Cost Percentage

Month	Music and entertainment (U.S. dollars)	Revenue (U.S. dollars)	Music and entertainment %
January	2,000	54,000	3.70
February	2,000	61,000	3.28
March	2,000	72,000	2.78
April	2,000	24,500	8.16
May	2,000	36,300	5.51
June	2,000	70,000	2.86
Average	2,000	52,967	3.78

Although other expenses percentages, taken individually, are generally much lower than the prime cost, the combination of total controllable and non-controllable other expenses can represent between *5 and 15 percent* of total sales in a food and beverage department.

Review questions

1. What are recipe costing cards used for?
2. Explain the difference between attainable and actual cost of sales.
3. Which are food and beverage's major security concerns?
4. What are the objectives of food and beverage cost control?
5. Which are the three phases of food and beverage cost control?
6. Which industry best practices may reduce beverage cost of sales?
7. List two examples of non-controllable expenses.
8. What is a variable expense?
9. Which are major security concerns in the kitchen?
10. Why should random inventories be carried out? By whom?

Exercises

Based on the following end of the month information, calculate the food cost percentage,

Food and beverage sales	$500,000
Food sales	75% of total sales
Beverage sales	25% of total sales
Beginning food inventory	$25,000
Ending food inventory	$30,000
Total food purchases	$200,000
Employee meal cost	$6,000

Classify the following expenses:

Other expenses	Variable expense	Fixed expense
Linen washing		
Fridge compressor repair		
Insurance premium		
Garbage removal		
Water bill		
Stationary used for menu printing		

Using the following information and cost prices from your local market, create your own recipe sheet.

Establish the attainable cost, and suggest a selling price for the dish.

Thai green curry with vegetables
Ingredients
1 spoon of green curry sauce
Green curry paste
4 bamboo strips
12 pieces of long green beans
2 pieces of cooked sweet potato
1 piece of eggplant, cut lengthwise
Kaffir lime leaf
3-4 julienne strips of red chili
1 tablespoon of coriander and Thai basil paste
Place a ladle of curry sauce on and small pan and heat on stove Add all the vegetables Season with fish sauce and add 1 tablespoon of curry paste Bring to boil and serve in a curry bowl

Bibliography

Davis, B., A. Lockwood, I. Pantelidis, and P. Alcott. 2012. *Food and Beverage Management*. Routledge.

Cichy, R.F., and P.J. Hickey, Jr. 2017. *Managing Service in Food and Beverage Operations*. American Hotel and Lodging Educational Institute.

Walker, J.R., and J.E. Miller. 2015. *Supervision in the Hospitality Industry*. Wiley.

Baker, K. 2000. *Project Evaluation and Analysis for Hospitality Operations*. Hospitality Press.

Kotas, R., and C. Jayawardena. 1994. *Profitable Food and Beverage Management*. Hodder and Stoughton Educational.

Dittmer, P.R., and J. Desmond Keefe. 2009. *Principles of Food, Beverage, and Labor Cost Controls*. John Wiley and Sons.

Glossary

Audit
Process whereby a manager compares the inventory that has been used with the
actual consumption

Average check
Mean amount of money spent per customer during a given financial accounting
period. Computed for food and beverage sales

Average spent
See average check

Bistronomy
Restaurant trend combining fine-dining cuisine and bistro-style service

Brigade
Organizational hierarchy for professional kitchens organized by the legendary
French chef, Georges-Auguste Escoffier

Budget
Projection of future sales and expenses. May be determined by dollar sales and
guest count, using sales history

Buffet
Dining offer where the guests serve themselves, and featuring a great variety of
products, which are attractively presented

CapEx
Capital expenditure. Purchases that will increase the value of the restaurant or
hotel, for example, kitchen equipment

Carving
Carvery is a type of assisted service, performed on a guéridon by a chef de rang

Casual
Informal style of restaurant

Catering
Activity or business providing food and beverage services for events

Chafing dish
Hollow ware used to keep the food warm usually in buffet service. Chafing dishes may be fuel or electric heated

Chef and dish
See chafing dish

Chinaware
Cups, plates, and bowls used in food and beverage service. Usually made of china

COGS
Cost of goods sold. The dollar amount of all food or beverage products used for the production of recipes

Conference
Event, which may last one or a few days, during which participants discuss a particular topic

Contracted service
Service proposed by a food and beverage operator to a private or public company, for example, a school or an airline

Controllable expense
Expense, which may be controlled or modified by the operator

Cost
See expenses

Cost provision
Expense budgeting system used by operators who have no possibility of raising their selling price for food and beverage items. For example, schools or similar institutions

Critical item
Food and beverage products of a high value and that are more exposed to theft or spoilage risks

Cutlery
Knives, forks, and spoons used for eating or serving food. Can be made of stainless steel or silver

D

Department
Part of an organization, such as a hotel or a restaurant, dealing with a particular area of work.
For example, the food and beverage department

Dispense bar
Bar that operates in the back of the house, out of guest's view

Distributor
Vendor purchasing directly from sources and reselling to customers

E

Executive committee
The management team of a hotel. Made of the general manager and the heads of
    departments or division heads: rooms division director, director of food and
    beverage, executive chef, director of sales and marketing, director of finance,
    director of maintenance

Expense
Cost associated with the running of a business, including the cost of sales, wages,
    and other costs

F

Fast food
Also named quick-service restaurants, mass-produced food with a strong priority
    placed on the speed of service

Fileting
To cut a piece of meat or fish from the bones

Financial period
Start and stop dates for a business period. For example, one month for the profit
    and loss report

Finishing kitchen
Also known as satellite kitchen. Used when space or location does not allow for
    a fully-fledged production kitchen. Preprocessed ingredients are prepared to
    order, assembled, and immediately sent out for consumption in the dining
    room

Food porn
Widely spread food and beverage trend, characterized by the provocative
    representations of food through photos, which are posted online. For
    example, *Instagrammable dishes*

Formula
Set menu, usually offered at lunchtime, at a medium price. Formulas may include
    starter and main course, or main course and dessert

Franchise
Business form where the owner, the franchisor, allows the operator (franchisee)
    to use his or her operating procedures and commercial name for a fee

G

Glassware
Glasses and other objects made of glass or crystal

I

Incomplete shipment
Delivery that misses some of the items ordered by the buyer

Intermediary
Another term for vendor

Inventory
Counting and valuation of products held in stores

K

Kickback
Illegal rebate or gift given by a supplier to a buyer, in exchange for exclusive
   purchase from the supplier

Kitchen pass
Stainless steel counter in the kitchen, where cooks place prepared dishes to be
   picked up by waiting staff

L

Locavorism
Food and beverage trend that promotes consumption of food products grown
   locally

M

Managed services
See contracted services

Management
Set of controls and organizational principles within a company

Menu analysis
Analysis of menu items' sales performance, in number of units sold and level of
   profitability

Michelin guide
Worldwide known culinary guide created in 1900 by the Michelin brothers.
   A reference in the culinary world

Michelin starred
Restaurant, which has been awarded one, two, or three Michelin stars

Mise en place

French term that means, *putting in place*. Preparation of a work place for trouble-free service

N

Non-controllable expense

Expense that may not be modified by the operator, such as income taxes for example

O

Operating cost

Day-to-day expenses associated with the running of a business

Operating equipment

Equipment that is used in day-to-day food and beverage operations. For example, kitchen equipment or service trays

Operations

Sum of business activities in a hotel or restaurant venture

Organization

Company arranged in groups of people sharing common goals and objectives

Outlet

Business entity within the food and beverage organization

Overheads

See expenses

P

Par stock

Widely used term in the hospitality industry: standard way to determine minimum quantities of products in order to ensure a smooth operation at all times

Pest control

Management methods to regulate the species defined as pests: rats, mice, insects. Under the responsibility of the chief steward

POS

Point of sale system, controlling hospitality operations' sales and product consumption by using a dedicated hardware and software

Prime cost

Combined costs of goods sold and labor cost, expressed as a percentage of sales

Producer
Primary source supplier, such as a farmer or winegrower

Production
Kitchen team in charge of the production of meals

Profit and loss
Detailed listing of revenue and expenses for a given accounting period. Also referred to as an income statement

Profit margin
Difference between the selling price and the cost of sales associated to a product or service

Profitability
Dollars remaining after all expenses have been paid. Often referred to as net income

Q

Quality
Of a high standard: this is a quality product or service

R

Ratio
Relationship between two amounts. One of food and beverage's main ratio is the COGS

Recipe costing sheet
Training and valuation tool used in food and beverage to calculate the attainable cost of recipes

Revenue
Term used to indicate the dollars taken in by the business in a defined period of time. Often referred to as sales

Roster
Employees' weekly working schedule, prepared by management

Rota
See roster

S

Seat rotation
Average amount of time that a seat is occupied by a guest

Set menu
Predetermined menu, often served during banquets

Shelf life
Amount of time a product can remain in storage

Short order
See incomplete shipment

Shrinkage
Inappropriate loss or theft of food and beverage products

Side station
A service stand in the restaurant that holds services supplies and equipment for easy access by waiters or waitresses

Sourcing
Purchase practices aimed at finding, evaluating, and selecting food and beverage suppliers

Standard
SOP: Acronym for standard operating procedure. Procedure specific to the operation, for example, an SOP for telephone answering

Stocktaking
See inventory

Supply chain
Flows of materials, goods, and related information among suppliers, company, resellers, and final consumers

T

Tableware
Tableware includes cutlery, chinaware, glassware, and linen

Trend
A new development in food and beverage practices

Turnover
Another term for *sales* or *income*

U

Upselling
A sales technique used by servers to increase guest satisfaction and sales by encouraging guests to order extras like starters, cocktails, desserts, and so on

Utilities
Expenses such as electricity, gas, water, sewage, and garbage removal

V

Veganism
Practice of not eating or using animal products

Viennoiseries
Refined pastry products such as croissants, served mainly during breakfast

W

Walk-in fridge
Refrigerator with doors through which personnel, trolleys, and carts may enter

About the Author

Sylvain Boussard is a Lausanne Hotel School graduate. He started his professional career in 1992, with a focus on international luxury hotel management, holding various management positions in a dozen countries such as Mexico, Peru, Brunei, and the Maldives.

In 2014, he joined the Le Cordon Bleu school in Paris, in order to develop a restaurant management program for postgraduate students interested in opening their own ventures. This year marked the beginning of his activities in the academic field, which continued in 2016 in St. Petersburg, Russia, as director of hospitality studies for Swissam hotel school.

In 2018, he created his own consulting company, *Biyahi Hospitality Expertise*, and initiated a professional blog *Hospitality, food and beverage, travel stories, https://hotels-food-travel.com*.

Sylvain Boussard also lectures and participates in conferences for various management schools in Paris and the Riga Hotel School in Latvia.

LinkedIn: www.linkedin.com/in/hospitalityeducation/

Website: BIYAHI – hospitality, food, and beverage expertise, www.hotels-food-travel.com/

E-mail: Biyahi@pm.me

Index

Concise and Applied Business Books

The Collection listed above is one of 30 business subject collections that Business Expert Press has grown to make BEP a premiere publisher of print and digital books. Our concise and applied books are for...

- Professionals and Practitioners
- Faculty who adopt our books for courses
- Librarians who know that BEP's Digital Libraries are a unique way to offer students ebooks to download, not restricted with any digital rights management
- Executive Training Course Leaders
- Business Seminar Organizers

Business Expert Press books are for anyone who needs to dig deeper on business ideas, goals, and solutions to everyday problems. Whether one print book, one ebook, or buying a digital library of 110 ebooks, we remain the affordable and smart way to be business smart. For more information, please visit www.businessexpertpress.com, or contact sales@businessexpertpress.com.

www.ingramcontent.com/pod-product-compliance
Lightning Source LLC
Chambersburg PA
CBHW061211220326
41599CB00025B/4601